Praise for *Power Over Addi*

"This excellent workbook will be of real value to anyone who wants to change the way they use drugs -- whether they want to quit, reduce, use more safely, or just better understand what drugs mean and do for them. The exercises won't always be easy, but they will help people get to the heart of their relationship with drugs, giving them more power to make choices they are happy to call their own."
-Hanna Pickard, PhD, Professor in Philosophy of Psychology, University of Birmingham and Visiting Research Scholar,Program in Cognitive Science, Princeton University

"...the workbook is filled with thoughtful and penetrating questions that will make it not only effective for those struggling with problematic drug use, but useful for anyone who wants to incorporate positive changes in their life."
-Monique Tula, Executive Director, Harm Reduction Coalition

"Jennifer Fernández, PhD has written a wonderful book of exercises for people who practice harm reduction. They include exercises for mindfulness, relationships, boundaries, anger, stress, shame, and many more. I highly recommend this book to all HAMS members as a companion to the HAMS book as well as to anyone who uses drugs or alcohol."
-Kenneth Anderson, CEO, HAMS Harm Reduction for Alcohol and author of *How to Change Your Drinking: A Harm Reduction Guide to Alcohol*.

"Dr. Fernández's new workbook is an incredibly welcome addition to the tools available for those struggling with substance use. She has made "harm reduction" a set of ideas and strategies that could benefit anyone, and assembled a set of strategies that pull from many evidence-based approaches including motivational, behavioral, and mindfulness based approaches. The strategies are accessible, practical, and geared toward real behavior change. I particularly love the "Note to Loved Ones" sections throughout the book, which offer compassionate and helpful tips to families struggling to know how to help in real ways."
-Jeffrey Foote,Ph.D., Co-Founder & Executive Director, Center for Motivation and Change and author of *Beyond Addiction: How Science and Kindness Help People Change*.

"...a wonderful addition to the growing body of resources for helping people who struggle with problematic drug use and their families make positive change with drugs and the personal and relationship issues problem drug use reflects. Dr. Fernández combines state-of-the-art knowledge about theories of addiction and how people change with practical user-friendly suggestions and exercises that guide people toward their ideal relationships to drugs. The harm reduction frame makes this workbook useful for people at all motivational stages of change and positive change goals including safer use, reduced use, and abstinence. Mindfulness and compassion inform the book's approach to supporting people in becoming more aware, self-caring, and empowered in relation to themselves and their lives. I highly recommend that this book sit within close reach on the shelf of every drug user and those who care about them."
-Andrew Tatarsky, PhD is the author of *Harm Reduction Psychotherapy: A New Treatment for Drug and Alcohol Problems* and the founder and Executive Director of the Center for Optimal Living, a treatment and professional training center in New York City based on his Integrative Harm Reduction Psychotherapy.

"If you have a loved one suffering from addiction, you should read this book. If you're a treatment provider working with people suffering from addiction, you should study this book. If you're a politician drafting addiction-related legislation (because I know you don't read), you should speak with Dr. Fernández immediately."
-Dr. Carl Hart, Chair of the Department of Psychology at Columbia University and the Dirk Ziff Professor of Psychology in the Departments of Psychology and Psychiatry and author of *Drugs, Society and Human Behavior* and *High Price: A Neuroscientist's Journey of Self-Discovery That Challenges Everything You Know About Drugs and Society.*

"This incredibly helpful workbook is a welcome addition to a growing goldmine of harm reduction resources in the U.S. In an inviting and clear style, Dr. Fernandez offers the reader a wealth of information about drug use and the contextual, mental, emotional, and physical issues that are part of a drug-using life. She takes a balanced perspective on the ways that drugs are valuable and the ways they can be harmful to each person. This point of view helps to relieve the shame and stigma that surround drug use. Dr. Fernandez covers a phenomenal number of self-awareness and practical skills that one needs to change longstanding patterns. The chapters are concise and the exercises easy to use. All of this makes *Power Over Addiction* a delight to read and use."
-Jeannie Little, LCSW, Executive Director of The Center for Harm Reduction Therapy

"This compassionate and easy-to-read workbook can help you or a loved one learn to change—or end— a problematic relationship with substances. There is hope— and this book can help you figure out what path is right for you."
-Maia Szalavitz author of *Unbroken Brain: A Revolutionary New Way of Understanding Addiction.*

Power
Over
Addiction

A Harm Reduction Workbook for Changing Your Relationship with Drugs

Jennifer Fernández, PhD

INVISIBLE
WORK
PRESS

Cover and text design by Terran Collective, LLC http://www.terran.io/
Artwork by Frizz Kid https://www.redbubble.com/people/thefrizzkid

Library of Congress Control Number: 2018902233
ISBN: 9781732032408

Contents

Foreword

It is always great to be able to welcome a new book that is rational, philosophical, and practical all at the same time. When that book is about drug and alcohol use, it's incredibly exciting as well. Dr. Fernández has added to a growing list of resources for people who are looking for a more compassionate, less shaming, and more successful method to deal with problems that have come about because of drug use.

I have been working in this field and developing harm reduction psychotherapy for over 40 years and Dr. Fernández was part of my mission to train new therapists in this model. She worked with clients under my supervision for three years and has been moving forward since then with her own career development. This book is one of her accomplishments, one that I hope I had some contribution to.

Based on the philosophy of harm reduction, Dr. Fernández takes the reader through a journey of self-discovery and change by allowing all of the components of drug use and drug problems to be held under a mirror. While other books in the self-help genre can seem simplistic, hers is rich in information and complex ideas. She engages the reader in exercises that they will actually want to do!

The book begins by talking directly about resistance, that "bad boy" of traditional drug treatment. Dr. Fernández makes it clear that resistance to change is normal and not something to be ashamed of or gotten rid of without examining how it both helps and hurts people in their efforts to change. This begins the format and style of the entire book: acceptance that people have complicated relationships with drugs; that people manage their feelings and behaviors in ways that can be helpful in the short run, but not so much in the long run (and vice versa!); that we all have cherished values that we may have forgotten or abandoned along the way to a serious drug problem; and that our very way of thinking about our relationship with drugs can be so skewed that we end up just feeling bad about ourselves, and powerless to change.

Dr. Fernández explains how drugs can become our partners, our best friends, or our strongest relationships. She then helps the reader analyze what is helpful or harmful about these relationships. This brings the reader's conflicts about changing into the real world and, as we make changes, leads us to a process of grieving for that old relationship.

A topic that is always talked about in books on drug use problems, but never in such a complete and helpful way, is how to manage urges and cravings. Clearly relying on her professional training in Cognitive Behavioral Therapy, Dr. Fernández designs a road map for the reader to see exactly how they get from a feeling to a behavior, from a trigger to a craving, and the whole jumble of thoughts and emotions that are part of this process. She reminds us that what we call cravings start as just a wish to do/feel something different in response to a situation (a trigger).

Dr. Fernández ends this incredibly smart and useful book with concrete examples and strategies about how to develop a safer and more satisfying relationship with drugs, where by moderating or abstaining.

Patt Denning, PhD
Director of Clinical Services and Training
Center for Harm Reduction Therapy

Preface

After many years of working with people who use drugs and their families, the need for a harm reduction workbook became clear. There are many resources available to people who want to abstain from drug use. Unfortunately, for those wanting to moderate or who are ambivalent about changing their relationship to drugs, sources of support are few and far between.

Not only are there insufficient psychoeducational resources like books and workbooks, but the vast majority of treatment programs are abstinence-only. My hope is that this book not only helps people who want to change the way they use drugs, but also inspires treatment providers to practice harm reduction therapy. Addiction treatment is not one-size-fits-all. People need options, especially options founded in pragmatism and compassion.

I started working on this book over a year ago. It has required the support and help of many people in the field of addiction treatment and in my community. Thank you to everyone who helped with the creation of this resource.

This project wouldn't have been possible without the guidance of my teachers and mentors. Patt, thank you for introducing me to the harm reduction community. Your passion for treating addiction is contagious! Samantha and Elizabeth, thank you for your ongoing support and wisdom. You have been incredible role models. I hope to have many more opportunities for learning from you.

My deepest gratitude goes to the hundreds of people I've worked with over the years. You have reached out for help and hope, sometimes in your deepest, darkest hour. Loved ones have reached out to find support or information for their partners, mothers, fathers, sons, daughters, uncles, aunts, or cousins. Together we have worked towards relief, recovery, and safety. Through that process, I've learned so much about addiction, trauma, shame, grief, and love. You've shown me the darkest corners of the human experience and inspired me with your courage to radically change. Thank you for choosing me to keep you company along the way. I dedicate this work to you.

Introduction

Who This Workbook is For

This workbook is for people who want to have healthy, responsible relationships with drugs. It can also be helpful for those who want to abstain from drug[1] use. People in all stages of the recovery process can learn from the concepts presented here.

This workbook is for you if:

- you've tried to have a different relationship with drugs in the past and it didn't work
- you're changing your relationship with drugs for the first time
- you want to stop using drugs
- you've been sober for a long time and want to establish a healthy relationship with drugs
- you're not sure whether you want to keep using drugs or not
- you want to learn about responsible drug use
- you're curious about the recovery process because someone you love is struggling with addiction

Learn how to have a healthy relationship with drugs

The information and exercises presented here are useful for any recovery process, regardless of the end goal. Sometimes people choose moderation as a goal and end up changing their goal to abstinence. And vice versa, someone who initially sets a goal for abstinence may change their mind and choose to moderate. Either way, this workbook can be helpful to you.

Understand addiction and recovery

Professionals and loved ones will also find this workbook useful for understanding addiction, the recovery process, and the skills necessary to overcome addiction. Throughout the chapters you will find sections of information specifically for you.

---

[1] A note about language: throughout this workbook I refer to all substances that alter consciousness as drugs, including alcohol and nicotine.

How to Use This Workbook

Commit to completing the exercises

This is hard work! Sometimes you will feel like quitting. This is normal. Find a way to keep going. It can be tempting to skip the exercises but completing them will add to the benefits of completing this workbook. The exercises provide a form of active learning, which has been proven to improve long-term memory of new information. For those who learn best from "doing" rather than "reading" it's a good way to apply the concepts in the book to your personal situation.

Most people find that having an accountability buddy helps them stay committed to their goals. Find someone at your local peer support group, like SMART Recovery or AA/NA who will check in with you about your progress on the workbook. Clergy members, trusted colleagues, a therapist, close friends, and family members are other potential sources of accountability buddies.

Remind yourself why you started this process. Give yourself healthy rewards. Splurge on a bouquet of flowers, take yourself out to dinner, go to a movie, schedule an hour for doing absolutely nothing, or watch your favorite show for the evening. Small rewards add up to bigger returns. You will feel more motivated to keep up with the hard work it will take to form a new relationship to drugs.

At first you may need to give yourself small rewards frequently: weekly bubble baths, shooting hoops every Wednesday and Sunday, daily affirmations of your accomplishments. Over time, give yourself bigger rewards spaced out over longer periods of time: treat yourself to a baseball game after not binge drinking for two weeks, take a spa day after reducing your cannabis use for a month, go out of town for the weekend after abstaining for three months.

When I feel like giving up I will ….

Place post-it notes throughout the workbook with this and other reminders.

When I feel like giving up I will call a trusted friend to encourage me to keep going.
When I feel like giving up I will remind myself why I want to make a change.
When I feel like giving up I will reflect on the progress I've made.
When I feel like giving up I will remind myself that I'm worth it.

Some other prompts you might find helpful:

I need to change because...
I'm doing this hard work because...
When I change my relationship to drugs I honor...
I deserve to have a better relationship to drugs because...

Set calendar reminders with these statements in the weeks and months to come. Make sure the notification is visible to you throughout different days of the week and at different times throughout the day. You may find it helpful to set multiple reminders on days when you are most likely to use problematically.

Don't feel limited to words

Use the margins and spaces throughout the workbook to draw or sketch your reactions to the material and exercises. Our automatic thoughts and reactions contain important information. **Document what you think, how you feel, and what you notice in your body as much as possible.** Journaling is highly recommended. You might choose to keep a notebook or sketchpad in addition to using this workbook.

Share what you learn

Teaching is a great way to learn new things. Talk to others about what you're learning. This doesn't necessarily mean disclosing personal information. Rather, report facts and objective information to interested parties. For instance, you might share what you learn about healthy boundaries with your coworker. Your friend might find it interesting to learn about cultivating a fulfilling lifestyle. Compare notes on mindfulness with someone who has their own meditation practice.

Get support

Some people are able to change their relationship drugs on their own. However, getting support from others will make the process easier. We are social creatures. We thrive on relationship. Find others who are also undergoing this process. Attend a local peer support group like SMART Recovery, AA, NA, or Life Ring. Join a therapy group. Enroll in a meditation class.

The chances of successfully moderating after problematic drug use are greatly improved with support from a professional. You will get more out of the concepts in this workbook with the help of a therapist or counselor. Call your insurance company and get a list of local addiction providers. Search the web for clinicians in your area. Get referrals from community members who have changed their relationship to drugs.

Set a consistent time every week to work on the exercises

We learn best and retain information more effectively when we study at the same time in the same place. Pick a time when you know you will be free every week and commit to working on the exercises then. Once you've got a date and time put it in your calendar. Work in a quiet, safe space.

Sometimes the exercises will be painful and you may want to cry. Crying is a natural process when we are grieving. Giving something up, even if it isn't working for us anymore, understandably arouses feelings of grief. Make sure the space where you're working is comfortable enough to express whatever emotions may come up.

Take as much time as you need

Again, this is a challenging process. You may find some chapters easy, others painful. Practice patience and compassion with yourself. And commit to keep the practice going. Make sure you're working on the exercises or practicing recovery skills every week, even if you find yourself reviewing material you've already covered.

Concepts are presented in a sequential order in the workbook so it's best to complete a chapter before moving on to the next. If you skip around, you may find some of the later exercises more difficult to complete.

What is Harm Reduction?

Do you wear a seatbelt? Wear a helmet when you ride a bike? You are practicing harm reduction!

Harm reduction emerged in the 1970s as a better health practice to reduce infection rates of HIV, AIDS, and hepatitis. Since then, it has also become a topic of advocacy among equal rights activists as well as medical and mental health professionals. Aside from reducing the negative consequences of drug use, harm reduction also aims at spreading awareness about the effects of drug use and ending the discrimination drug users are subjected to from employers, doctors, government, and society.

Harm Reduction Psychotherapy is addiction treatment specifically suited for people with co-occurring psychiatric disorders and histories of trauma. It differs from traditional abstinence-based treatment in that clients do not need to be "clean and sober" in order to receive services. Instead, clinicians work with clients to identify the benefits and consequences of drug use and make changes to improve their quality of life. It has also expanded to include a psychotherapeutic treatment option to reduce harm associated with behaviors other than drug use, such as body dysmorphia, sex addiction, and other impulse control disorders.

Many believe Harm Reduction Psychotherapy is opposed to abstinence-based treatment, but abstinence is a goal that many clients choose. In fact, abstinence is the best form of harm reduction!

Harm Reduction Psychotherapy helps people increase self-efficacy and reduce negative consequences related to drug use by applying theories of motivational interviewing, psychodynamics, and cognitive-behavioral strategies.

Note to Professionals

If you would like to use this workbook with clients, please have them purchase a copy. Contact me directly for information about reduced cost materials for community mental health agencies or educational materials.

I strongly recommend *Harm Reduction Psychotherapy: A New Approach to Drug and Alcohol Problems* by Andrew Tatarsky, PhD and *Practicing Harm Reduction Psychotherapy* by Patt Denning, PhD and Jeannie Little, LCSW. If you haven't already, read these books before beginning this workbook with your clients.

Seek out group or individual consultation if you are new to Harm Reduction Psychotherapy. Cynthia Hoffman, MFT offers trainings and facilitates a professional consultation group on Harm Reduction Psychotherapy in the San Francisco Bay Area. Patt Denning, PhD and Jeannie Little, LCSW also consult with individuals and community-based organizations. Please contact me for information about individual consultation and supervision.

Always recommend a medical examination when beginning treatment with a new client. Drug use has an affect on our bodies and physical health is essential to mental health. Active drug users should check in with their primary care provider on a yearly basis if in good health and more frequently if they have physical health issues.

Note to Loved Ones

Bearing witness to a loved one's addiction can be incredibly painful. Make sure you're getting support from others while you support your loved one during recovery. *SMART Recovery* has online and in-person meetings for friends and family. Visit http://smartrecovery.org/resources/family.htm for more information. And of course there's also *Al-Anon* (http://al-anon.org/find-a-meeting) and Nar-Anon (http://nar-anon.org/find-a-meeting).

I highly recommend *Beyond Addiction: How Science and Kindness Help People Change* by Jeffrey Foote, PhD, Carrie Wilkens, PhD, and Nicole Kosanke, PhD and *Over the Influence* by Patt Denning, PhD and Jeannie Little, LCSW. These books provide excellent information about addiction and the recovery process and offer solutions for loved ones affected by addiction.

If your efforts to help your loved one have been unsuccessful, I recommend seeking your own therapy. It may seem strange to start your own treatment process, especially if you're not "the one with the problem," but caregiver burnout is a risk for loved ones. Some of you may feel very alone with the struggle of loving someone with an addiction. Therapy can help you identify healthy sources of support, healthy boundary setting with your loved one, and prevents isolation.

Chapter 1
The Truth About Addiction

 "What is addiction, really? It is a sign, a signal, a symptom of distress. It is a language that tells us about a plight that must be understood."
-Alice Miller

Addiction is a **biopsychosocial phenomenon** that results in negative consequences including feelings of shame and guilt. Biological, psychological, and social factors culminate into a dependent relationship with a drug or compulsive behavior as a means of coping with distressing emotional, psychological, and environmental states.

More specifically, addiction is characterized by several criteria:

1. the inability to resist an urge to consume a drug or engage in a behavior that is harmful
2. an increase in tension or arousal before the act, followed by gratification and relief
3. a noticeable increase in amount and frequency of the act in order to achieve the desired effect (e.g. pleasure or escape)
4. over-investment of resources, such as time and money, to engage in the act

The emotions associated with addiction are one of the most notable elements. Shame, guilt, and powerlessness are hallmarks of addiction and often lead to feelings of self-loathing and isolation. Individuals suffering from addiction are often misunderstood by their families and loved ones, causing them to lie and keep secrets.

Informing yourself can be the first step in gaining power over your addiction.

Addiction affects over 20 million people in the United States. The factors that cause addiction are not yet well understood — some researchers argue that it is a brain disease while others suggest it is more like a syndrome. However, we can identify some predictors for addiction and we do understand the impact it has on the brain, on people, and on society.

This chapter will primarily focus on current understanding about the brain structures and neurotransmitters involved in addiction. We'll also look at the interaction that specific drugs have with neurotransmitters in the brain and how this accounts for preferences in drug selection. We'll start with an overview of addiction theories then dive into the neurocircuitry and neurobiology of addiction. We'll conclude by looking at the effect of drugs on neurotransmitters in the brain and discuss why one develops a drug of choice.

Theories of Addiction

Although we don't fully understand addiction, there are lots of theories that attempt to explain it. A **moral model** of addiction dominated the mainstream before science informed our understanding of it. It suggests that people with addiction make bad choices and should be judged for them. It adheres to beliefs like, "Once an addict, always an addict" and maintains that people with addiction are selfish, lazy, untrustworthy, and criminal.

The new mainstream understanding of addiction is the **disease model**. It explains that addiction has a biological origin that causes changes in the brain. It asserts that people with addiction cannot stop themselves from using because their brain is different. This model also accounts for the heredity of addiction, or genetic predisposition. Studies of twins who have been separated at birth show that they are likely to develop addictions, despite growing up in different home environments.

You may have also heard that addiction hijacks the reward center of the brain. Brain imaging studies show that chronic, problematic use of drugs or compulsive behaviors "hijack" the reward system and can lead to changes in the brain that make it difficult to experience pleasure.

Recently, there has been more focus on challenging the disease model of addiction, since it is evident that people can and do make the choice to stop using problematically. Carl Hart, PhD a professor of psychology and psychiatry at Columbia University who studies addiction has shown that people addicted to crack will make rational choices, like choosing $20 later over a hit of crack now.

Some experts regard addiction as a **learning disorder**. Addictive behavior interferes with decision making and motivation. Once a pattern of behavior is repeated enough times it becomes locked in or automatic. This continues despite no longer being adaptive because the behavior fulfills a psychological purpose. As with other learning or developmental disorders some people may have a predisposition to addiction, meaning the way their brain is wired makes them more vulnerable. To learn more about addiction as a learning disorder read *The Biology of Desire* by Marc Lewis, PhD and *Unbroken Brain* by Maia Szalavitz.

Hanna Pickard, PhD a professor of philosophy of psychology at the University of Birmingham proposes a new conceptualization of addiction: **Responsibility without Blame**. She believes addiction is a choice that people can stop making under the right circumstances. This model holds people accountable for their choices, but does not judge or stigmatize behavior.

Then there's the **self-medication hypothesis**. It suggests that people use drugs to help them cope with physical and/or emotional pain. It helps explain why people turn to specific drugs or compulsive behaviors to help them deal with depression, anxiety, chronic pain, trauma, or grief.

Perhaps the best way to explain addiction is as a **biopsychosocial phenomenon**. We know that addiction has a biological component. It causes temporary and permanent changes in the brain and body. We also know there are psychological components: inability to cope with distressing emotions, low self-worth, unmet needs due to an inadequate lifestyle. The social component of addiction is related to the dominating cultural messages about drugs, the influence of peer culture over what drug to use, how to use it, or how (not) to deal with emotions. It also relates to the way systemic oppression affects people and their access to resources for coping.

In the question about nature versus nurture, the answer might just be nature *and* nurture. Drugs affect us biologically and we may even be genetically predisposed to those effects. Plus, your parents, family, friends, or lovers may have modeled addictive behaviors or inability to cope with emotions in a healthy manner.

The Neurocircuitry of Addiction

Addiction causes changes to brain structures that regulate pleasure, motivation, and decision making. Depending on the type of drug abused and the length of the abuse, these changes can be permanent. Other factors, such as pre-existing differences in brain structure (like depression, schizophrenia, or ADHD) can also make the effects of drug misuse irreversible. The primary brain structures affected by drug use and compulsive behaviors are the ventral tegmental area (VTA), the nucleus accumbens, and the prefrontal cortex.

This is your brain

The VTA is the birthplace of dopamine, a chemical that signals the brain about pleasure. It is involved in cognition, motivation, learning, intense feelings of love, addiction, and psychiatric disorders.

The nucleus accumbens (NA) is the reward and pleasure center of the brain. Depending on the message, it sends dopamine to various areas of the brain. Permanent changes occur to this brain structure with repeated drug use. These changes explain drug tolerance (needing to take more drugs to feel high) and drug withdrawal (physical and psychological discomfort when drug use stops abruptly). The NA is also involved in fear, aggression, laughter, impulsivity, and learning.

The prefrontal cortex (PFC) is the part of the brain that makes us different from other animals. It is responsible for executive functioning which involves complex brain functions such as differentiating from good and bad or same and different, identifying future consequences, predicting expectations based on actions, working towards a goal, and suppressing urges that might be deemed socially unacceptable. In the brain of addicted individuals, the PFC is thought to be involved in anticipation of the drug, motivation to seek out the drug, craving, automatic responses to emotions, and reduced self-control. Once a person becomes addicted their attention narrows to focus on drug-related cues over all other reinforcers, impulsivity increases, and basic emotions become unregulated.

This is your brain on drugs. For real.

Addiction is scary. It has caused pain in many people's lives and has cost families and governments trillions of dollars to treat and prevent. It's no surprise that social service agencies want to educate the general population about the harms of addiction. You may have seen the public service announcement comparing an addicted brain to fried eggs. The image is powerful, yes, but it is not educational. This is what actually happens in your brain when you take drugs.

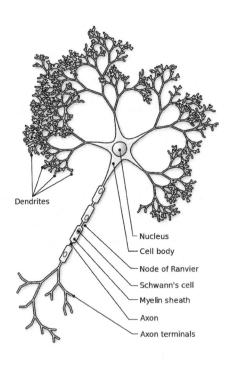

Image by Nicolas Rougier

Above is an image of a neuron. The brain is filled with billions of these nerve cells and supporting structures. They contain genetic information and also serve as messengers. They transmit information through fibers from one cell to another via electrical charges. Neurons generate messenger chemicals, or *neurotransmitters*, to transmit information from cell to cell. The electrical charge travels through the dendrites, cell body (or soma), axon, and terminal bud down to the synapse — the gap between neurons where the magic happens.

Neurotransmitters live in the terminal bud of neurons. An electrical charge comes through the neuron and releases the messenger chemicals. The chemicals then float across the synapse and attach to the neighboring cell for a short amount of time in a process called *neurotransmission*. Once the message has been relayed, they return to their home cell. This process is called *reuptake*. For example, if you were to burn your hand on the stove, nerve cells in your muscles would send a message to the neurons in your brain saying, "Ouch!" This alerts your brain to release endorphins, the brain's natural pain reliever. The endorphins do their job and relieve the pain long enough so you can think to run cold water over your hand. Once the message has been communicated, the endorphins return to their home cell until the next electrical charge commands them to be released.

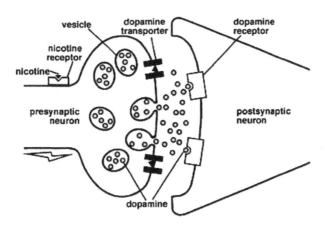

Image by the National Institutes of Health

Above we have a close up of the synapse (the gap between neurons) and what happens there when nicotine is present in the brain. The neurotransmitter dopamine has been released into the synapse to send a message to the neighboring cell. Once dopamine has completed its task, it attempts to go back home, but nicotine is blocking the way of the dopamine transporter route. Since dopamine can't go back home it goes back to doing its job, binding to the neighboring cell. Dopamine's loitering, so to speak, is what causes feelings of intense pleasure and euphoria.

Neurotransmitters and Addiction

Dopamine is just one of dozens of neurotransmitters. It is the most well known chemical messenger and is responsible for feelings of pleasure, coordination of movement, and logical thinking. It is responsible for the rush one feels when they engage in a compulsive behavior or use a recreational drug. It also influences the addictive potential of a behavior or drug. It is released when we do things that are important for survival, like sleeping, eating, and having sex. Dopamine sends the message, "That feels good! Do it again!"

This is your brain on dopamine

Dopamine is a neurotransmitter responsible for movement, pleasure, motivation, and cognitive processes, such as learning. For the purposes of understanding its role in addiction, let's concentrate on pleasure and motivation.

Whenever we do something that propagates the advancement of our species, dopamine is released in order to motivate repetition of the action. When we sleep, eat, and have sex dopamine is released in the brain and the message is, "That was great, do it again!" We also release dopamine whenever we find something pleasurable. Be it 18th century poetry, heroin, or electronic music, **the brain will release dopamine to identify the behavior as something that brings us pleasure.**

Dopamine not only serves to categorize the good things we encounter in life, it also programs our pre-frontal cortex (the part of the brain involved in judgement and decision making) to alert us when the pleasurable stimulus is available. If your brain cells could talk, it might sound something like, "OMG! There's a flyer on that lamppost for a Radiohead concert. Go look at it!" In other words, we become hyper aware of opportunities for engaging in behaviors that bring us pleasure. In fact, a study on people with alcoholism found they were more likely to spot alcoholic beverages in a busy photograph than people who don't have problems with alcohol.

When we consume drugs or engage in compulsive behaviors, we feel good because the brain releases dopamine. But drugs cause a higher amount of dopamine release than is necessary. This is part of what creates experiences of euphoria and feeling high.

Sometimes the amount of dopamine released is so great or frequent, the chemicals in the brain become unbalanced and we may experience hangover or withdrawal. Over time, the brain regains chemical equilibrium. However, if one misuses drugs the brain may develop a tolerance (meaning the person needs to use greater amounts to get high) or dependence on the drug as a source of dopamine. If one becomes dependent on a drug, it will take time for the brain to regain equilibrium and the person may experience extreme physical discomfort and emotional distress when they aren't using.

The period of recalibration depends on the amount, type, and frequency of the drug used. **It's**

always a good idea to be under medical supervision and receive support from friends, family, and a mental health professional if you're dependent on a drug and want to stop or decrease your use. In some cases (such as with alcohol and benzodiazepines) withdrawal can lead to death.

The mechanism of tolerance is also evident in impulse control disorders, such as sex addiction, kleptomania, and compulsive gambling. Although it doesn't appear that people with an impulse control disorder undergo the same intensity of withdrawal than those addicted to drugs, there will certainly be a period of recalibration of dopamine receptors during which a person feels irritable and agitated after stopping a behavior.

Based on the information presented here, it may appear as though we are all hardwired to develop addiction and you may be asking yourself, "If this is true, why do some people become addicted and others don't?" This is a really good question and the answer is that we don't really know. We have been able to identify risk factors such as first age of drug use and family history of addiction. We also know that a lack of social support and coping strategies (especially when coupled with mental illness) can lead to addiction, but there is no conclusive answer to date.

The best ways to prevent addiction are to educate ourselves about the drugs we use (or to abstain from drug use altogether) and to be mindful about the choices we make. If one has a mental illness, ensuring that they are getting appropriate treatment and maintaining social support are good preventative measures.

Other Neurotransmitters

Norepinephine is one of the brain's natural stimulants. It is responsible for increased alertness and focus, is involved with learning and memory processes, and is a key target in the treatment of depression. Norepinephrine is also involved in the fight or flight response. It signals the release of adrenaline in the body to prepare for survival in the face of imminent danger. It sends the message *Fight!* or *Run!*

GABA (gamma-aminobutyric acid) is the brain's Valium. It relaxes the brain by suppressing overexcitement or hyperactivity, while remaining alert and focused. Low levels of GABA are associated with anxiety and seizure.

Glutamate stimulates various activities throughout the brain, especially for learning and memory. We don't know much about how it is involved in mood regulation.

Serotonin plays several complex roles in the brain. It is involved in regulating mood, sleep, appetite, and sex drive. Low levels of serotonin are associated with aggression, irritability, and depression. Serotonin plays a role in the effects of psychedelic drugs.

Endorphins are the brain's natural opioids. They influence the perception and control of physical and emotional pain. In addition to pain relief, they are responsible for feelings of well-being, happiness, and euphoria.

Drugs act on these messenger chemicals to increase, decrease, or alter their release or reuptake. The brain is wired to recognize these chemicals and accept their messages. The difference is that drugs relay the message better, faster, and in a much more intense way.

Research shows that life experiences affect the development of the brain, including how neurotransmitters work. For example, someone who has experienced trauma may find it difficult to feel pleasure or regulate their mood due to low levels of dopamine and serotonin. This may cause them to turn to externally supplied chemicals to balance the levels of neurotransmitters in their brain.

Developing a Drug of Choice

Drug of choice can say a lot about a person or what they're coping with. People choose drugs that will best help them cope with underlying problems. Sometimes these problems include severe mental illness. Addiction can occur when drugs or compulsive behaviors are relied upon for alleviation from multiple or serious problems.

Alcohol is often sought out by those who have a hard time expressing themselves, especially if coupled with social anxiety. It makes one feel loose and carefree by releasing GABA and suppressing glutamate in the brain. The soothing and disinhibiting effects are also helpful to people in emotional pain, such as someone suffering from grief. Sometimes people with trauma histories turn to alcohol to soothe their psychological wounds. People with schizophrenia sometimes use alcohol to quiet auditory hallucinations.

Amphetamines give you a rush of pleasure and boost energy and focus by altering norepinephrine and dopamine in the brain. They may be sought out by someone who is depressed and has been unable to feel pleasure for some time. Improved focus may be sought after by someone with ADHD. Antipsychotic medication can have dulling and flattening side effects and sometimes people with schizophrenia seek out the alertness and energy of stimulants. Nicotine is used by 95% of people with schizophrenia because of its ability to increase concentration and focus.

Opioids may help someone who is feeling irritable, stressed, or moody by blocking endorphin receptor sites in the brain and increasing feelings of euphoria. People who have experienced trauma or are in significant emotional pain may also turn to opioids to help soothe and forget their painful memories. Trauma survivors may also turn to dissociatives (such as ketamine) for their ability to induce out of body experiences.

MDMA and other empathogens create a sense of connection, emotional openness, feelings of warmth, and empathy by altering serotonin and norepinephrine receptor sites. Someone with anxiety or an inability to feel pleasure may turn to this class of drugs for comfort. MDMA is currently being studied for use with trauma-related disorders and preliminary results shows it to be an effective treatment for reducing symptoms of Posttraumatic Stress Disorder.

Recreational and pharmaceutical drugs work on the same systems in the brain. If your drug use is an attempt to self-medicate an underlying problem, speaking to a trained professional can help you find healthier alternatives to cope.

Note to Loved Ones

I hope what you've just read about addiction helps you better understand what your loved one is going through. Addiction is really complex and the person dealing with it wants to be free from it just as much as you want them to be.

I'm often asked, "What can I do to help my loved one realize they have a problem?" Chapter 2 on change offers more guidance on how to help based on the stage of change your loved one is in. When a person doesn't recognize they have a problem, the best support we can give them are compassion and understanding.

When a person is in denial, the most effective strategies to help them change are expressing our concerns and reflecting what we see. If your loved one is struggling at work or in their relationships, let them know you see it and offer support for those problems. Do so as compassionately and nonjudgmentally as possible.

Remember, there is nothing you can do to make them change. They have to want to start the change process themselves. Your words of encouragement and loving concern can help move that process along. But ultimatums, threats, or force won't. In fact, the chances of treatment success for mandated patients are low. A classic intervention where the person is confronted about their problem will likely only lead to shame and increased problematic behaviors.

Letting your loved one know how you really feel about their addiction can also help. Chapter 6 on communication can help you put together your thoughts and feelings in order to communicate effectively and compassionately.

The most important advice I can give is to take care of yourself. Addiction and mental illness place a big toll on caregivers. If you aren't caring for yourself, how can you care for another? Make sure you are getting the support you need to address the impact that addiction is having on you. Join a support group. Go to therapy. Make sure you're spending some time NOT thinking about addiction or your loved one.

Sources

Center for Behavioral Health Statistics and Quality. (2016). *Key substance use and mental health indicators in the United States: Results from the 2015 National Survey on Drug Use and Health* (HHS Publication No. SMA 16-4984, NSDUH Series H-51). Retrieved from http://www.samhsa.gov/data/

Hart, C. (2013). *High Price: A Neuroscientist's Journey of Self-Discovery that Challenges Everything You Know About Drugs and Society.* New York, NY:Harper.

http://www.drugpolicy.org/drug-war-statistics

Lewis, M. (2015). *The Biology of Desire: Why Addiction is Not a Disease.* New York, NY: PublicAffairs.

Lunza, K. (2016). Mandatory addiction treatment for people who use drugs: global health and human rights analysis. *British Medical Journal*, 353. DOI: https://doi.org/10.1136/bmj.i2943

Pickard, H. (2017). Responsibility without Blame for Addiction. *Neuroethics*, 10(1): 169-180. DOI: 10.1007/s12152-016-9295-2.

Szalavitz, M. (2016). *Unbroken Brain: A Revolutionary New Way of Understanding Addiction.* New York, NY: St. Martin's Press.

Recommended Reading

Denning, P. & Little, J. (2017). *Over the Influence* (2nd ed.). New York, NY: The Guilford Press.

Foote, J; Wilkens, C; Kosanke, N; & Higgs, S. (2014). *Beyond Addiction: How Science and Kindness Help People Change.* New York, NY: Scribner.

http://www.stuartmcmillen.com/comic/rat-park/

Meyers, R. & Wolfe, B. (2003). *Get Your Loved One Sober: Alternatives to Nagging, Pleading, and Threatening.* Center City, MN: Hazelden Publishing.

Chapter 2
The Change Process

We typically think of change as a linear process. It is anything but.

Change is a slow, incremental process. Relapses, setbacks, and mistakes are part of the change process and are, in fact, essential. **Without mistakes we are unable to learn.** Though the point of a relapse prevention plan is to avoid relapse, most people will relapse many times throughout their recovery process.

Relapse is an opportunity to learn. When we are unable to meet a goal, there is a lot of information we can analyze that helps us determine our needs and limitations. **Instead of seeing relapse as a failure, see it as an opportunity.**

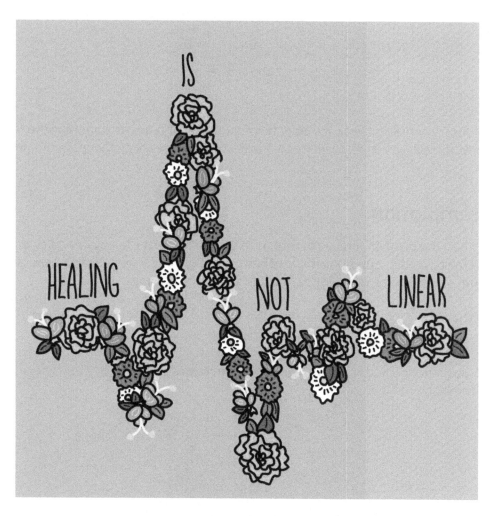

Stages of Change

The stages of change developed by Prochaska and DiClemente provide a simple framework to help us think about the change process. The five stages are:

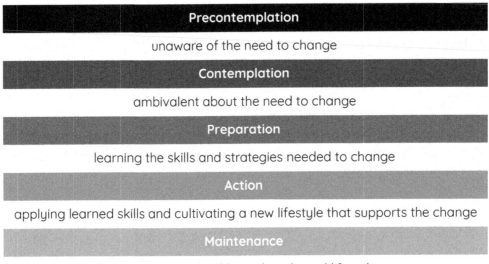

Precontemplation
unaware of the need to change

Contemplation
ambivalent about the need to change

Preparation
learning the skills and strategies needed to change

Action
applying learned skills and cultivating a new lifestyle that supports the change

Maintenance
maintaining a healthy, values-based lifestyle

Again, since this process isn't linear, it's more helpful to think of these as stations rather than stages. In this framework, relapse acts as a vehicle that takes us back to earlier stations in the process.

Precontemplation

During this stage, the person is unable to recognize their problematic behavior and change isn't considered. Efforts to point out problematic behaviors are ignored, rejected, and dismissed. Feedback from others seems exaggerated, misdirected, or controlling.

This stage is the toughest for loved ones. The most effective strategies for loved ones to implement at this stage are:

1. reiterate concerns and worries in a compassionate way
2. set healthy boundaries

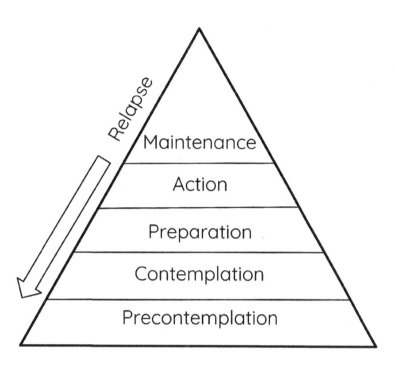

Continued repetition of a loved one's concerns can sometimes illuminate ambivalence between a person's values and their behaviors which will help move them along to the next stage. Until the person struggling with addiction experiences compelling consequences (either internal or external) change will not occur. **The desire to change needs to come from within.** Therefore, strategies like interventions or sending the person to rehab are likely to fail at this stage.

Contemplation

This stage is really the springboard for the rest of the change process. Ambivalence and dissonance are the hallmarks of this stage as the person starts to acknowledge to themselves and others that there are problems associated with their behavior. They can also acknowledge the benefits of their relationship to drugs. This is the best time to start working with a professional or getting support from others.

Identifying the benefits of one's relationship to drugs provides crucial information about the issues underlying addiction and the healthy alternatives that will become part of a healthier lifestyle.

At this stage an intervention or consultation with a licensed professional who can provide compassionate and evidence-based information about addiction can be helpful. The professional can assess the person's readiness to begin treatment and help loved ones identify the most effective strategies for supporting someone through recovery.

It is important to remember that awareness of consequences may be fleeting. There are many factors that can push a person back into precontemplation. They may cycle back and forth between the first two stages of change for some time. When the ambivalence is resolved and the person feels supported they will move into preparation.

Preparation

Most people completing this workbook are in the preparation stage. They have identified a behavior they would like to change and are taking observable steps to do so. The preparation stage is about acquiring information and skills to stop a problematic behavior.

This stage can feel overwhelming. There is a lot of information to learn and lots of changes to make that lead to the end goal. It is important to take as much time as needed in this stage. Loved ones can be supportive by practicing patience and offering lots of praise and words of encouragement. The person undergoing change should expect to come back to preparation even after they've put things into action. **The process of learning about oneself is lifelong.**

Action

The action stage may be challenging, but will also feel great. The skills and knowledge acquired during preparation are put into place to create a values-based lifestyle. The person might feel like they're in the flow. They will also likely encounter obstacles and challenges as new strategies are implemented, therefore ongoing support is required.

At this stage a person might feel like stopping therapy and pulling away from their support system. **It may feel like the work is done, but in some ways it is just beginning.** Make a commitment to getting the support you need. Loved ones can continue to offer praise, words of encouragement, and reflection of the person's progress.

Maintenance

At this point, the desired change has been sustained for some time. A healthier lifestyle is in place. There is no longer shame about their relationship with drugs. There is increased confidence in addressing the stressors that life brings. A process for coping that is aligned with one's values has been developed. One feels content with themselves and their relationships. Loved ones no longer feel concern and may feel more connected.

Relapse

Relapse can occur at any point throughout the change process. It is defined as a behavior that a person would like to avoid. For those who want to stop using drugs, relapse is defined as any use. Those who want to form healthy relationships with drugs define relapse as problematic use.

As you can imagine, problematic use looks different for everyone. Be sure to define relapse for yourself and be open to changing the definition over time. For example, a person may first define problematic drug use as drinking to blackout. Over the course of developing a healthy relationship to alcohol, they may choose to only drink to the point of feeling buzzed and define drunkenness as problematic.

It is normal to feel shame, guilt, and a sense of failure after a relapse. Practice patience and compassion with yourself after engaging in problematic use. Remember that each setback is an opportunity to learn something about your change process, your relationship with drugs, and yourself.

Ponder This...

How did you respond to concerns about the addiction when you were in the precontemplation stage?

_____

_____

_____

How did you talk to yourself about the addiction during the precontemplation stage?

_____

_____

_____

Which stage are you currently in and how do you know?

_____

_____

_____

Each setback is an opportunity to

learn about my needs and limitations.

What behaviors have you successfully changed in the past? How can you apply what you learned from that change process to this one?

_____

_____

_____

What behaviors were you unsuccessful at changing in the past? How can you apply what you learned from that change process to this one?

_____

_____

_____

How are you defining relapse right now?

_____

_____

_____

List five things your support group can do right now to help you change.

1.

2.

3.

4.

5.

Exercise: Decisional Balance

A decisional balance is a pros and cons list about changing a behavior. Although it may be easier to focus on the consequences, think especially hard about the benefits. How do you feel when you use? What do you gain from your relationship to drugs? Remember, you wouldn't have such a committed relationship to it without good, compelling reasons.

Complete the decisional balance below, paying extra attention to the benefits and listing as many of them as possible.

Decisional Balance	
Costs of Relationship to Drugs	**Benefits of Relationship to Drugs**

Now look at the benefits and rank them by importance on a scale from one to five where:

1 = not at all important
2 = somewhat important
3 = important
4 = very important
5 = essential to my well-being

Exercise: Finding Alternatives

Now that you're familiar with the benefits of your relationship with drugs, let's identify some alternatives that achieve the same goal. Make sure to identify both quick fixes and long-term solutions to use when you feel the urge to use but don't want to. The quick fixes will be very useful as you begin resisting urges to use.

In the first column of the table list all the gains (or benefits) you identified from the last exercise. For example, you may gain a feeling of escape, happiness, social interaction, or confidence.

In the second column list other ways you can gain the benefit. Remember that people and places can act as sources of benefits, too. Maybe there's a place in your neighborhood or your house where you feel escape or a friend with whom you feel very safe and confident.

Don't feel limited by activities or external coping strategies. Identify your internal resources as well. Try mindfulness, imagery, or positive self-talk. As you learn new skills from this workbook add them to this table.

In the last column, indicate whether the alternative is a long-term solution (LT) or quick fix (QF). Aim for alternatives in each category.

Alternative Strategies		
What I gain from using	Other ways to gain the benefit	LT/QF

Exercise: Goal Setting

Now let's determine your drug use goal. You may have already decided to moderate your relationship with drugs or maybe you are unsure which strategy is best for you. Complete a decisional balance for moderation and another for abstinence. What are the costs and benefits of each of those drug use strategies?

Decisional Balance for Moderation	
What I stand to lose from moderating	What I stand to gain from moderating

Decisional Balance for Abstinence	
What I stand to lose from abstaining	What I stand to gain from abstaining

Look through the benefits and consequences and rank them by importance from one to five where:

1 = not at all important

2 = somewhat important

3 = important

4 = very important

5 = essential to my well-being

How do these ranked lists inform your drug use goal?

_____

_____

_____

How might you be minimizing any of the gains or losses?

_____

_____

_____

What did you notice when completing the table for moderation versus abstinence? What thoughts, emotions, or body sensations did you experience?

_____

_____

_____

Write about any resistance you may have noticed to this exercise. What do you think it means?

_____

_____

_____

Note to Loved Ones

Think about behaviors you have changed or tried to change in the past. Were you able to do so without relapsing? How many tries did it take before you were able to sustain the change? Are there goals that you gave up on because they were too difficult to achieve?

It will be important for you to celebrate each incremental change you notice. No change is too small. Make sure your loved one knows you notice the work they're doing. It is very easy for a person to become discouraged during the change process. It's hard work. Be the best cheerleader you can be for your loved one. And accept that this won't always be an easy task.

Help your loved one combat feelings of shame. Remind them they are lovable, valuable, and needed. Validate how challenging change can be. Empathize with their struggle. Don't try to fix it or sugar coat it. Name it: *Gosh, changing relationships to drugs is such hard work.*

Practice *yes, and...* and avoid *yes, but...*

Yes, this is super challenging and I will be right by your side the whole time.
Yes, this feels awful and I want you to tell me all about it.
Yes, you relapsed and I want to help you learn from it.

During the precontemplation stage, you will likely need to set new boundaries with your loved one. The point of the boundary should be to protect yourself, not to punish your loved one. **Punishment does not help addiction, it exacerbates it.**

You may want to set boundaries around money, time, shared spaces, and the way you interact with your loved one. Setting healthy boundaries prevents caregiver burnout and models healthy behavior for your loved one.

If you feel resentful that your money is being spent on drugs, stop giving money to your loved one and pay for the items or services they need directly. If you are worried your loved one will steal from you to purchase drugs, lock your valuables in a safe.

If you feel uncomfortable or unsafe when your loved one is using, let them know. If they are unwilling or unable to stop using in your presence, you will have to make arrangements to remove yourself from the situation. Let your loved one know why you are leaving: *I feel scared when I see you high, so I'm going to spend the night at my friend's house tonight.* Notice how this is about you and not them.

Sources

Prochaska, J., Norcross, J., & DiClemente, C. (1994). *Changing for good: the revolutionary program that explains the six stages of change and teaches you how to free yourself from bad habits.* New York, NY: W. Morrow.

Chapter 3
Cultivating Mindfulness

"Our life is an endless journey: the practice of meditation allows us to experience all the textures of the roadway, which is what the journey is all about."
- Chögyam Trungpa Rinpoche

You may have heard the buzz about mindfulness and its benefits. In fact, it's true that mindfulness has a positive impact on one's physical and mental health and it will become a very important part of having a healthier relationship with drugs.

What is Mindfulness?

Many people immediately think of meditation as a form of mindfulness, but there are many ways to be mindful. You probably already practice mindfulness in your everyday life.

Mindfulness means sustained attention. There are many opportunities to focus our attention throughout the day. Driving, biking, and walking require our undivided attention. Chopping vegetables or frying eggs requires us to focus on the task at hand. Of course, the mind will wander while participating in these tasks and that's just the brain doing its job. A wandering mind is a normal human function.

Mindfulness practices teach the mind to redirect focus. In some meditation practices, attention is focused and redirected to the breath. When the mind becomes distracted, the practitioner redirects their attention to the act of breathing: inhalation, exhalation, the pause in between, the depth of breath, its quality, how the breath is experienced in the body.

The point of meditation is not to clear the mind, but rather to redirect it. Clearing the mind is not possible for more than a moment at a time. As one becomes more skilled at their mindfulness practice, they are able to sustain focus for longer periods of time.

Another important aspect of mindfulness is nonjudgment. Practicing meditation or any other mindfulness practice can become frustrating as the mind will wander, requiring you to redirect your attention. When this happens, practice patience and compassion. Don't judge your thoughts or reactions while practicing mindfulness. Instead, see if you can access gratitude towards the aspects of your mind that try to pull you away from the present moment.

Mindfulness cultivates discernment, the ability to make informed observations based on a deeper understanding or knowing. Most of the time the mind responds automatically to stimuli. Mindfulness helps us slow these responses down in order to respond intentionally versus automatically. This skill will help you have a better relationship to yourself and the world around you.

Why is mindfulness important in recovery?

Cultivating mindfulness is important in any recovery process as it will help you make different choices. It will help you respond to urges with intentional and value-based decisions. It will help you maintain healthy rituals for drug use. It will help you make decisions about which drugs to ingest and the amounts to take. Mindfulness is about being in relationship with yourself, your environment, and those around you.

In *The Mindful Brain* Dan Siegel suggests that mindfulness requires curiosity, openness, acceptance, and compassion. These attitudes will come in handy when changing your relationship to drugs.

When you notice a desire to use, practice curiosity. Ask yourself why you want to use. Identify the benefits and potential outcomes sought by using. How do you imagine you will feel about yourself after using? Are you trying to escape or avoid something by using? Be really curious about it.

Openness and flexibility will help you make the lifestyle changes necessary to have healthy relationships with drugs. Remain open to different possibilities and outcomes. If you notice an urge to use, be open to alternatives. What else will help you achieve or comes close to the desired benefit? Open your mind to different beliefs and attitudes about the reasons you use. It's ok to escape unpleasant feelings sometimes. We're only human, after all. How can you be open to trying new, healthy ways of escape?

Mindfulness is also about acceptance. Accept that pain is part of the human experience. Accept that you will not always meet your drug use goals. Accept that others will disappoint you. **Radically accept that you have worth and limitations.** Acceptance of what we cannot control is simultaneously terrifying and liberating. Accept yourself as you are in this moment. If you notice a desire to use, accept that sometimes you may not be able to overcome it. Make a choice to use in a safe way. Accept that setbacks are part of the change process. Accept that coping will sometimes be challenging. Accept that doing this is hard!

Above all, be compassionate with yourself. It is hard, challenging, and vulnerable work to change one's relationship to drugs. Remind yourself of that fact. Reward yourself in healthy, nurturing ways. Acknowledge there are parts of you that are scared, tired, hurt, and in need of relief. Acknowledge how your choices impact the people you love. Your relationship to drugs may hurt or scare them. Have compassion for them as well.

Mindfulness Exercises

These are only a few of many different types of mindfulness practices. The internet is a wealth of resources on the topic including information, videos, books, and lectures. If you think you want to try meditation, sign up for a class, look for videos online, or check out apps. Be skeptical of sources that claim to be "the way" to mindfulness. Remember that physical activities are a great source of mindfulness, too. The point is to maintain sustained focus while minimizing distractions.

Practice a mindfulness exercise at least once a day. Take notes in your journal about your experiences to help you reflect on the best type of mindfulness practice for you.

Sensate Focus

This mindfulness practice involves using your five senses to practice sustained attention. It can be helpful in gaining a few minutes of relief from distressing thoughts, urges, or feelings. You will need a timer and 10 minutes for this exercise.

See

Take a moment to see your surroundings. Look deeply and intentionally. Set a timer for two minutes and list every object within your field of vision. If your mind becomes distracted, return to naming the objects you see.

Hear

Reset the timer for two minutes. Close your eyes and list everything you hear. Are there cars rumbling outside? Birds chirping? An old pipe creaking? Can you hear yourself breathing? Can you hear your heart beating?

Smell

Take a deep breath. Close your eyes. Now another deep breath. What can you smell? Is the smell of soap lingering from your morning shower? Is a neighbor cooking dinner? Can you smell the laundry detergent in your clothes? Are fragrant flowers nearby? What about a trash can? Can you smell a fresh breeze through an open window? Take two minutes to identify as many smells as possible.

Touch

For two minutes, connect to your felt sense. How does the seat feel against your legs and back? What is the texture of your clothes against your skin? Do you have glasses on your face? Is your hair brushing your cheek? Is a fan or breeze blowing? Does your skin feel cool or warm?

Taste

This one can be challenging, but try your best. Focus on your sense of taste for two minutes. Is the taste of your lunch lingering on your tongue? If you're unable to register any taste, take at least one minute to notice the taste of your mouth. Is it salty? Sweet? Neutral?

Diaphragmatic Breathing

By engaging the abdomen while breathing, one can elicit a parasympathetic nervous response. This is the mechanism that relaxes the nervous system when it has been aroused. Practice this exercise when you're feeling angry, anxious, irritable, or having an urge to use.

On a scale of one to ten, one being the most relaxed you've ever felt and ten being a panic attack, rate your level of activation.

Inhale for a count of five seconds.

Hold your breath for a count of two seconds.

Exhale for a count of ten seconds.

Repeat at least five times.

Rate your level of activation on a scale of one to ten after completing the five cycles.

Hula Hoop

This imagery exercise will help release any tension or discomfort in your body due to stress, anxiety, or urges. You may want to make a recording of the instructions and play it back to yourself.

Imagine a hula hoop levitating over your head. As it lowers over your body, it scans for tension, tightness, discomfort, or activation and brings softness, heaviness, space, and relaxation to those areas.

As the hula hoop begins to lower over the forehead, notice a broadness behind the eyebrows and a release of the skin on the forehead.

The eyes move away from the eyelids and sink into their sockets.

The jaw becomes heavy. The upper and lower teeth move away from each other. The tongue moves away from the roof of the mouth and recedes towards the throat.

The skin on the neck melts down towards the floor.

The shoulders grow heavy and broad.

The chest becomes heavy and spacious.

The abdomen becomes soft and full.

The tops of the thighs become heavy and recede into the seat.

The muscles on the shins and calves melt towards the floor.

The feet are incredibly heavy and anchor into the ground.

Repeat as many times as necessary.

Wise Mind

In Dialectical Behavioral Therapy, the relationship between thoughts, feelings, and behaviors is examined to help people stop problematic behaviors. The mind is divided into three states: rational, emotional, and wise.

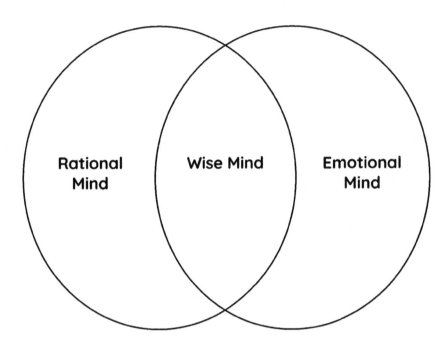

Rational mind is present when a person responds to a situation intellectually. They use logic and facts for planning, decision making, and to inform their behavior.

A person uses emotional mind when they allow their feelings to influence their thoughts and behaviors. They act impulsively and with disregard for consequences.

Wise mind is the middle ground between rational and emotional mind. A person is able to identify and respect their feelings while responding in a rational manner. They can interpret the message being communicated by their feelings, reality test their interpretation, and plan for an appropriate response. This way they are honoring their feelings while responding with healthy, adaptive behaviors.

Practice wise mind when feeling hot-headed or during an urge. Use a relaxation or grounding exercise to engage the parasympathetic nervous system. This will allow emotional mind to calm down and rational mind to come online.

Make an interpretation about your feelings. Why are you feeling this way right now?

_____

_____

_____

Ask what might be distorted about the initial interpretation. Is it exaggerated? Have you minimized it? Have you left out important information? Or added false evidence?

_____

_____

_____

After answering these questions and practicing curiosity and openness, make a values-based decision about how you'd like to respond.

_____

_____

_____

Ponder This...

Which of these mindfulness exercises will be most useful to you as you change your relationship to drugs? Why do you think so?

_____

_____

_____

_____

Sources
Linehan, M. (1993). *Skills Training Manual for Treating Borderline Personality Disorder.* New York, NY: The Guilford Press.

Recommended Reading
Siegel, D. (2007). *The Mindful Brain: Reflection and Attunement in the Cultivation of Well-Being.* New York, NY: W&W Norton & Company, Inc.

Kabat-Zinn, J. (1990). *Full Catastrophe Living.* New York, NY: Random House.

Chödrön, P. (2013). *How to Meditate: A Practical Guide to Making Friends with Your Mind*. Boulder, CO: Sounds True.

Chapter 4
Understanding Your Values

Values are the principles and standards by which we structure our lives. They inform how we live, who our friends are, and even the job we choose.

Values are central to who we are as individuals and form our personal truths. We tend to feel proud of our values and are willing to speak up for and defend them. **Understanding our values helps us make decisions that improve our wellbeing and quality of life.** When faced with a difficult decision, values are a helpful guide.

Values tend to remain relatively stable over time, but life experiences can sometimes change what we value. For example, in your early career you may have valued money but work-life balance may have become more important after you had a family. When life starts to feel unbalanced, it may be time to determine whether you are living in line with your values.

Values must be chosen freely. If you adopt a value because of its popularity or moral righteousness it will not necessarily add benefit to your life. There are no right or wrong answers here, so be honest with yourself while completing the exercises below.

When we are aware of our values and make choices aligned with them, life tends to be pretty good. But when we make choices that contradict or interfere with our values, life is distressing and unsatisfactory. Your values offer a lot of information and guidance when deciding what type of relationship you'd like to have with drugs.

Shame can be an indication that you are making choices outside of your value set. Keep in mind that shameful behaviors are usually an attempt to cope. Have compassion for the parts of you that need coping and challenge yourself to find alternatives that don't lead to shame. Consult with your values to determine the best alternatives for you.

It should be noted that we sometimes feel inappropriate shame after absorbing messages about who we should be. Because the messages are not in alignment with our values, they can result in feelings of shame. Some examples are homophobia, misogyny, racism, xenophobia, moral superiority, and classism.

Look through the list of values on the following pages and mark the ones that are most important to you.

(Exhaustive) List of Values

Ability Affluence Availability Abundance Aggressiveness Awareness **Acceptance** Agility Awe Accessibility Alertness **Balance** Accomplishment Aliveness Beauty Accountability Altruism Being-ness Accuracy Amazement **Achievement** Amusement Belief Acknowledgement Anticipation **Belongingness** Action Appreciation Beneficent Activeness **Approachability** Benevolence Adaptability Approval Blissfulness Adequacy Art Boldness Adoration Articulacy **Bravery** Adroitness Assertiveness Brilliance Advancement Assurance Briskness Adventure Attentiveness Buoyancy **Affection** Attractiveness **Calmness** Camaraderie Closeness Consistency Candor Cognizance Contemplation Capability Coherence Contentment **Care** Comfort Continuity Carefulness Commitment **Contribution** Celebrity Community Control Certainty Compassion Conviction Challenge Competence Conviviality Change Complacency Coolness **Charity** Competition Cooperation Charm **Composure** Copiousness Chastity Concentration Cordiality Cheerfulness **Confidence** Correctness Clarity Conformity Country Classiness **Congruency** Courage Cleanliness Connection Courtesy Clear-mindedness Consciousness Craftiness Cleverness Conservation Creativity Credibility Dignity **Economy** Cunning Diligence Ecstasy **Curiosity** Diplomacy Education Daring Direction Effectiveness Decisiveness Directness Efficacy Decorum **Discernment** Elation Dedication Discipline Elegance **Depth** Discovery Empathy Deference Discretion Encouragement Delicacy Diversity Endurance Delight Dominance Energy Dependability **Dreaming** Engagement Depth Drive Enjoyment Desire **Durability** Enlightenment Determination Duty Entertainment Devotion Dynamism Enthusiasm Devoutness Ease **Equality** Dexterity **Eagerness** Ethics Euphoria Fame Exactness Family Fortitude Excellence Fascination Frankness Excitement Fashion Freedom Exhilaration Fearlessness **Free-thinking** Expectancy Fierceness Freshness **Expediency** Fidelity Friendliness Experience Financial freedom **Friendship** Expertise Fineness Frugality Exploration Finesse Fun Expressiveness Firmness Gallantry Extravagance **Fitness** Generosity Extroversion Flexibility Gentility Exuberance Flow Genuineness Evolution Fluency Giving Facilitating Fluidity **Goodness** Fairness Focus Grace Faith **Forgiveness** Graciousness Gratefulness Humor Intelligence **Gratitude** Hygiene Intellect Gregariousness Imagination Intensity Growth Immovable

Intimacy Guidance Impact Intrepidness Happiness Impartiality **Introversion** Hardiness **Intuition** Harmony Independence Intuitiveness Health Individuality Investing Heart Industry **Inventiveness** Helpfulness Influence Involvement Heroism Informative Joy Holiness Ingenuity Judiciousness Honesty Inquisitiveness **Justice** Honor Insightfulness Keenness Hope Inspiration **Kindness** Hospitality Instinctiveness Knowledge Humility Integrity Lasting Lavishness Meekness Obedience **Leadership** Meaningfulness Objective **Learning** Mellowness Open-mindedness Legacy Mercy Openness Liberation Opportunity Liberty Mindfulness Optimism Lightness **Moderation** Opulence Liveliness Modesty Order Logic Motivation Organization Longevity Mysteriousness Originality Love **Nature** Outdoors Loyalty **Neatness** Outlandishness Majesty Neighborly Outrageousness Making a difference Nerve Partnership Malleable Nimble Passion Marriage Noble Patience **Mastery** Non-conformity Peace Maturity Nurturing Perceptiveness Potency Qualifications Performance **Power** Quietness Perkiness Practicality Quickness **Perseverance** Pragmatism Rationality Persistence Precision Realism **Personable** Preeminence Readiness Persuasiveness **Preparedness** Reason Philanthropy Presence Reasonableness Piety **Pride** Recognition Planning Privacy Recreation **Playfulness** Proactivity Refinement Pleasantness Proficiency Reflection Pleasure Professionalism Relaxation **Prosperity** Reliability Poise Prudence Relief Polish Punctuality Religion Politeness Purity Reputation Popularity Purpose **Resilience** Resolution Self-control **Skillfulness** Resolve Selflessness Smartness Resourcefulness Self-realization Sophistication Respect Self-reliance Solidarity **Responsibility** Self-respect Solidity Restfulness Self-sufficiency **Solitude** Restraint Sensitivity Sophistication Reverence **Sensuality** Soundness Richness Serenity Speed Rigor Service Spirit Sacredness Sexuality Spirituality Sacrifice Sharing **Spontaneity** Sagacity Shrewdness **Spunk** Saintliness Significance **Stability** Sanguinity Silence Status Satisfaction Silliness Stealth Science Simplicity Stillness Security Sincerity Strength **Structure** Thrift Valor Sturdiness **Tidiness** **Variety** Substantiality Timeliness Victory Success Togetherness Vigor Sufficient Toughness Virtue Superiority Tradition Vision Support Tranquility **Vitality** Transcendence Vivacity Surprise Tribe **Volunteering** Sympathy Trust Warm-heartedness Synergy **Trustworthiness** Warmth Tactfulness Truth Watchfulness Teaching Understanding Wealth Teamwork Unflappability Wholesomeness Temperance **Uniqueness** Willfulness Thankfulness **Unity** Willingness Thoroughness Usefulness Winning Thoughtfulness Utility Wisdom Wittiness Wonder **Worthiness** Youthfulness Zeal

Ponder This...

Where did your values come from? Who or what influences which values you keep, discard, or amend?

_____

_____

_____

How do disadvantages impact the ability to live your values? For example, lack of access to education may have prevented you from pursuing your dream job.

_____

_____

_____

Values Journaling Exercise

Assessing our values is a lifelong practice and ultimately leads to increased quality of life. Use the list of core values and this journaling exercise to help you identify yours.

For each category, circle to indicate its importance, why it's important to you, how much time you dedicate to it, and its ideal expression.

Don't feel limited by the categories presented here. Complete the journaling exercise for values not listed here, too.

FAMILY	How important is it?	Not at all important	Somewhat important	Important	Very important	Essential to my well-being
	Why is this value important to you?					
	What percentage of your time goes towards this goal? What gets in the way of contributing more?					
	What do you need to contribute an appropriate amount of time to this value?					
	What makes for an ideal family?					

How important is it?	Not at all important	Somewhat important	Important	Very important	Essential to my well-being
Why is this value important to you?					
What percentage of your time goes towards this goal? What gets in the way of contributing more?					
What do you need to contribute an appropriate amount of time to this value?					
What makes for an ideal friendship?					

FRIENDS

SIGNIFICANT OTHER	How important is it?	Not at all important	Somewhat important	Important	Very important	Essential to my well-being
	Why is this value important to you?					
	What percentage of your time goes towards this goal? What gets in the way of contributing more?					
	What do you need to contribute an appropriate amount of time to this value?					
	What makes for an ideal partner?					

How important is it?	Not at all important	Somewhat important	Important	Very important	Essential to my well-being
Why is this value important to you?					
What percentage of your time goes towards this goal? What gets in the way of contributing more?					
What do you need to contribute an appropriate amount of time to this value?					
What makes for an ideal job?					

W O R K

How important is...	Not at all important	Somewhat important	Important	Very Important	Essential to my well-being
creating beauty?					
creating ideas?					
making things?					
managing people?					
organizing things?					
performing physical tasks?					
responsibility?					
independence?					
leisure time?					
money?					
possessions?					
power?					
prestige?					
security?					
structure?					
improving society?					
helping people?					
following directions?					
experiencing variety?					

LEISURE	How important is it?	Not at all important	Somewhat important	Important	Very important	Essential to my well-being
	Why is this value important to you?					
	What percentage of your time goes towards this goal? What gets in the way of contributing more?					
	What do you need to contribute an appropriate amount of time to this value?					
	What are ideal forms of leisure?					

MEANING OR SPIRITUALITY	How important is it?	Not at all important	Somewhat important	Important	Very important	Essential to my well-being
	Why is this value important to you?					
	What percentage of your time goes towards this goal? What gets in the way of contributing more?					
	What do you need to contribute an appropriate amount of time to this value?					
	When do you know your life is meaningful?					

COMMUNITY	How important is it?	Not at all important	Somewhat important	Important	Very important	Essential to my well-being
	Why is this value important to you?					
	What percentage of your time goes towards this goal? What gets in the way of contributing more?					
	What do you need to contribute an appropriate amount of time to this value?					
	What makes for an ideal community?					

	How important is it?	Not at all important	Somewhat important	Important	Very important	Essential to my well-being
H	Why is this value important to you?					
E A	What percentage of your time goes towards this goal? What gets in the way of contributing more?					
L T	What do you need to contribute an appropriate amount of time to this value?					
H	What is your ideal picture of health?					

ACHIEVEMENT	How important is it?	Not at all important	Somewhat important	Important	Very important	Essential to my well-being
	Why is this value important to you?					
	What percentage of your time goes towards this goal? What gets in the way of contributing more?					
	What do you need to contribute an appropriate amount of time to this value?					
	What are ideal forms of accomplish-ment?					

How important is it?	Not at all important	Somewhat important	Important	Very important	Essential to my well-being
Why is this value important to you?					
What percentage of your time goes towards this goal? What gets in the way of contributing more?					
What do you need to contribute an appropriate amount of time to this value?					
What are ideal ways to care for the planet?					

CARING FOR THE ENVIRONMENT

CONCERN FOR OTHERS	How important is it?	Not at all important	Somewhat important	Important	Very important	Essential to my well-being
	Why is this value important to you?					
	What percentage of your time goes towards this goal? What gets in the way of contributing more?					
	What do you need to contribute an appropriate amount of time to this value?					
	What are ideal ways to care for others?					

CREATIVITY	How important is it?	Not at all important	Somewhat important	Important	Very important	Essential to my well-being
	Why is this value important to you?					
	What percentage of your time goes towards this goal? What gets in the way of contributing more?					
	What do you need to contribute an appropriate amount of time to this value?					
	What are ideal expressions of creativity?					

W E A L T H	How important is it?	Not at all important	Somewhat important	Important	Very important	Essential to my well-being
	Why is this value important to you?					
	What percentage of your time goes towards this goal? What gets in the way of contributing more?					
	What do you need to contribute an appropriate amount of time to this value?					
	What are ideal forms of wealth?					

	How important is it?	Not at all important	Somewhat important	Important	Very important	Essential to my well-being
L E A R N I N G	Why is this value important to you?					
	What percentage of your time goes towards this goal? What gets in the way of contributing more?					
	What do you need to contribute an appropriate amount of time to this value?					
	What are ideals ways to acquire new information?					

Ponder This...

Which values are being violated by your current relationship with drugs? Which values are being honored?

_____

_____

_____

Be honest. Can you honor your values while maintaining a relationship to drugs? Describe what you need in order to achieve it.

_____

_____

_____

Chapter 5
Forming Healthy Relationships

Humans are social creatures. We require relationship to have fulfilling lives. We develop relationships to people, other species, things, ideas, and behaviors.

Everyone has a relationship style they are most comfortable or familiar with. We interact in fearful, avoidant, anxious, or secure ways. Relationship styles are learned from our family of origin and change based on the environment, our mood, and the people with whom we are interacting.

Relationship Styles

Fearful

Fearful relationship styles regard both the self and the other as untrustworthy, damaged, unlovable, or unwanted. A person with a fearful attachment style may have experienced chronic trauma throughout their life and have a hard time trusting themselves and others in relationship. Because of this, there is little emotional intimacy and closeness in their relationships.

Avoidant

An avoidant relationship style is also characterized by distance. Generally the person adopting this style has a positive sense of self, but is skeptical of others. They may deem others as needy, intrusive, or smothering. It is hard for a person with this style to accept others' needs and boundaries.

Anxious

Anxious relationship styles are the flip side of an avoidant style. The self is viewed as damaged, unlovable, or lacking while the other is deemed to be exemplary, perfect, and ideal. This causes clinginess, excessive fear about abandonment, and codependency.

Secure

Secure attachment style is the healthiest way to be in relationship. There is acknowledgement of everyone's worth, strengths, and weaknesses. There is regard for one's own needs and boundaries and also for the other's well-being. Negotiation, vulnerability, and assertiveness are characteristics of this relationship style.

> In order to have healthy relationships with others, we need to have a healthy relationship with ourselves.

Since relationship styles are learned and fluid, the good news is that we can all become more securely attached in our relationships. This is hard work. We have to increase awareness about our relational patterns, unlearn these old styles of relating, and become more vulnerable about our needs and boundaries.

In order to have healthy relationships with others, we need to have a healthy relationship with ourselves. We need to understand our needs, wants, boundaries, and values. We need to communicate directly and develop empathy for others' needs.

Revisit Chapter 4 on values. Take what you've learned about your values and use this insight to identify an ideal romantic relationship. What are the characteristics of your ideal partner? What elements need to be present in order to have a healthy, secure romantic relationship?

The Ideal Relationship	
My Relationship Values	My Ideal Partner

Prioritize the elements of healthy relationship you've identified for yourself. Which elements must you absolutely have? In other words, identify the deal-breakers. These are your needs. Now, identify the elements that would be nice to have but are not essential to a healthy relationship. For example, it might be nice to have a partner who likes to travel but you can fulfill your desire to travel with friends or family. The nice-to-haves are your wants.

My Ideal Relationship	
My Relationship Needs (deal-breakers)	My Relationship Wants (nice-to-haves)

Ponder This...

Which relationship style did you adopt in your family while growing up? Think about whether you used different styles to attach to mom, dad, and siblings.

_____

_____

_____

As an adult, which relationship style do you use in romantic relationships? How about in your friendships?

_____

_____

_____

If you don't attach securely, what's getting in the way? What skills do you need to learn to become securely attached?

_____

_____

_____

Which relationship style do you use with drugs?

_____

_____

_____

Recommended Reading

Levine, A. & Heller, R. (2010). *Attached: The New Science of Adult Attachment and How It Can Help You Find — and Keep — Love.* New York, NY: Penguin Group.

Hendrix, H. (2008). *Getting the Love You Want: A Guide for Couples.* New York, NY: Henry Holt and Company, LLC.

Chapter 6
Tools for Effective Communication

 "What others do may be a stimulus of our feelings, but not the cause."

-Marshall B. Rosenberg, Ph.D.

Effective communication is essential for maintaining healthy relationships. In order for others to understand us, we need to be able to express our needs, boundaries, and feelings. We often romanticize others' abilities to read our minds and we sometimes long for others to fulfill our deepest needs without ever uttering a word about them, but this is unrealistic. Even a close friend or partner of many years cannot anticipate our needs, boundaries, or feelings. No matter how well you think someone knows you, it is important to speak up when you aren't getting something you need.

Communication Styles

Depending on our current state of mind, the environment, and with whom we are communicating we adopt one of four communication styles: aggressive, passive, passive-aggressive, or assertive.

Passive communication is avoidant and aims to not rock the boat. One withholds their feelings and needs but eventually builds resentment towards others. Aggressive communication is violent and can involve yelling, throwing things, name-calling, and hitting. A passive-aggressive communicator will deny their upset while engaging in aggressive actions. This includes intentional mistakes, backhanded compliments, sarcasm, deliberate procrastination, and sulking.

Assertive communication addresses one's feelings, needs, and boundaries. It facilitates mutual understanding and negotiation. It includes vulnerable statements: *I feel sad; I feel afraid; I need support; I want more of your time.* This communication style works best when all participants are actively open and honest. Empathy, trust, and respect are necessary elements for use of this communication style.

Ponder This...

Which communication style do you practice most often?

_____

_____

_____

What do you need in order to communicate assertively?

_____

_____

_____

Basic Building Blocks of Communication

Talk about yourself

Healthy communication is vulnerable communication. It requires self-awareness.

Healthy communication focuses on the self, not others. When communicating about the impact that a behavior had on you, make sure to begin your statements with "I".

I feel angry when you don't keep your promises. NOT _You're pissing me off! You never keep your promises._

I'm afraid you will fall out of love with me and leave. NOT _You're going to leave me. I know you don't love me._

The difference may seem subtle, but it makes a huge difference for the person on the receiving end. "You" statements sound like blame or accusation and can lead to defensiveness. The point of healthy communication is to ensure that everyone feels safe enough to share their inner experience.

Active Listening & Mirroring

Active listening is a form of mindfulness. It means hearing someone without preparing comparisons, comebacks, or arguments. The active listener must remain as present as possible with the speaker.

At times it may be difficult to understand the speaker. That's okay. It doesn't necessarily mean the communication is failing. It may be hard to empathize with the speaker's experience.

To build your empathic skills, practice mirroring. Mirroring is a communication technique where participants take turns being a sender and a receiver. It has two steps:
1. checking for accuracy
2. demonstrating understanding

The sender communicates their feelings, wants, needs, or boundaries while the receiver actively listens.

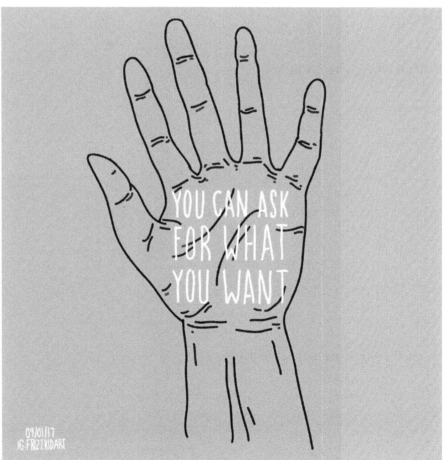

Once the sender has finished speaking, the receiver mirrors or repeats what they heard. Here the receiver is checking for accuracy to ensure they correctly heard the sender's message. At first, it may seem like you are just parroting back to the sender. That's okay. Over time the receiver will get better at paraphrasing. The point of this step is to ensure accuracy.

Next the receiver demonstrates understanding by expressing empathy for the sender. You might say something like, *I understand why you'd feel that way...* If the receiver doesn't understand and is having difficulty accessing empathy, ask for clarification. It's okay to say, *I don't understand why you feel hurt. Can you help me understand?*

Once the sender feels heard and understood, switch roles. As you can imagine, this type of communication takes a lot of work and can feel exhausting. Be intentional about it and give yourself adequate time and space.

I'm feeling upset about our last interaction. When can we schedule a time to have a dialogue about it?

I feel hurt that you mentioned the addiction in front of your co-workers. I need for us to have a moment about it. When's a good time for you?

Ponder This...

What's difficult about talking about yourself?

_____

_____

_____

What would make vulnerable communication less challenging for you?

_____

_____

_____

What's the most challenging aspect of active listening?

_____

_____

_____

Nonviolent communication

Nonviolent communication (NVC) is a great process for communicating in difficult situations. It involves self-compassion, empathy, and authentic expression. It challenges "right versus wrong" or the idea that conflict results when someone has "done something to us." By communicating nonviolently, we are able to resolve conflict without perpetuating pain.

NVC has four components: observations, feelings, needs, and requests.

1. Provide a factual observation of the hurtful action that took place. This means describing the event free from blame, criticism, or judgment.
When I heard you talking with your co-worker about my relationship to alcohol...

2. Name the feeling(s) that arose in response to the hurtful action.
...I felt hurt and confused...

3. Inform or remind the listener of your needs and values.
...because I need some privacy around this issue so I can address the shame I feel about it. I value having a strong sense of trust in our relationship.

4. Make a request. This is not a demand. Be as specific as possible and name a concrete, observable action.
Would you be willing to check in with me before talking to others about the addiction?

The listener can practice mirroring at this point to check for accuracy, demonstrate empathy, and respond to the request.

Exercise: A Month of Healthy Communication

1. Practice talking about yourself for a week. Start as many statements as possible with "I feel," "I need," and "I want."

"I" Statements			
Date	"I feel" statements	"I need" statements	"I want" statements

2. Practice active listening for a week. Keep a log for each day noting who you listened to, the topic, how long you listened, and how it felt to listen without responding.

Active Listening				
Date	I listened to...	talk about...	for...	and I felt...

3. Practice mirroring for a week. Start with easy, superficial topics. Mirror your co-worker after they complain about work stress. Mirror a loved one after they vent about chores or traffic. Gradually work your way up to more difficult conversations over the course of the week.

Mirroring				
Date	I mirrored...	and it was...		
		easy	challenging	very difficult
		easy	challenging	very difficult
		easy	challenging	very difficult
		easy	challenging	very difficult
		easy	challenging	very difficult
		easy	challenging	very difficult
		easy	challenging	very difficult

4. Practice nonviolent communication for a week. Again, start with easier topics and work your way up to more difficult or uncomfortable conversations over the week.

Nonviolent Communication				
Date	Hurtful Event	Feelings	Needs/Values	Request

Sources

Rosenberg, M. B. (2003). *Nonviolent Communication: A Language of Life.* Encinitas, CA: PuddleDancer Press.

Chapter 7
Healthy Boundaries

Boundaries are essential to healthy relationships. They keep us safe and define who we are. Boundaries acknowledge that each participant in a relationship is a whole person and separate from others. Although one might think of boundaries as rules of engagement, they are not rules to be imposed on others. Rather, boundaries are about you; your feelings, wants, and needs. Communicating your boundaries clearly is informative for others and minimizes assumptions, blame, and resentment.

Boundaries are fluid and evolve as we grow and learn about ourselves. Boundaries are also informed by setting (work versus home) and the people with whom we are interacting (co-worker, partner, person from a different cultural background).

Boundaries can be harsh, lenient, or healthy. Harsh boundaries keep others at a distance. Lenient boundaries lead to overinvolvement with others. Healthy boundaries allow us to say "no" when we need to, but also allow us to open up in close relationships.

Examples of Harsh, Lenient, and Healthy Boundaries		
Harsh	Lenient	Healthy
Avoidance of intimate relationships	Difficulty saying "no"	Understanding personal needs, wants, and values
Unwillingness to share vulnerably with others	Oversharing personal information	Valuing own opinions
Few close relationships	Accepting abuse or disrespect	Accepting "no" from others
Unwillingness to ask for help	Dependence on others' opinions	Unwillingness to compromise values for others
	Overinvolvement in other's problems	

Boundary setting is not always natural or easy. It takes lots of practice.

Creating healthy boundaries requires self-awareness and self-acceptance. You must believe that your worth and value aren't dependent on others. In order to identify your boundaries you must take the time to become aware of your feelings, needs, and relationship values.

Boundaries need to be communicated clearly and directly. We can't expect others to read our minds. Be specific. Use nonviolent communication. Take ownership of your needs. You may feel guilty, selfish, or embarrassed at first. Start small. With time, setting healthy boundaries will feel empowering.

Sometimes your boundaries will hurt or trigger others. This is a normal part of human relationships. Remember that you are not responsible for someone's reaction to a boundary. They have to take ownership of their response and remain accountable for communicating their feelings and needs.

Sometimes your boundaries will be violated. It is important that others understand the consequences for boundary violations. This is not to be mistaken for threats or ultimatums, but rather consequences for their decision making. Be sure to have reasonable and healthy consequences.

For example, you may choose to spend less time with someone or communicate mistrust after a betrayal. Anticipate a need for some time to go by in order to help with the reparation process after a boundary violation.

If a friend is irresponsible with borrowed items, it would be reasonable to stop lending them things. If a sibling shares intimate information with your parent without your permission, it would be reasonable to refuse sharing details with them. If a partner snoops through your phone instead of communicating assertively with you, it is reasonable to set a passcode. If someone wants more of your time than you're willing to give, it is reasonable to say no to their requests for your time.

Don't use manipulation to influence others. Vulnerability is more powerful at influencing others.

Signs of Unhealthy Boundaries

Talking about intimate subject matter with someone you just met
Falling in love with anyone who reaches out
Being sexual for your partner but not yourself
Going against personal values to please others
Not noticing when someone else displays inappropriate boundaries
Accepting food, gifts, touch, or sex that you don't want
Touching a person without asking
Taking as much as you can get for the sake of taking
Giving as much as you can give for the sake of giving
Allowing someone to take as much as they can from you
Letting others direct your life
Letting others describe your reality
Letting others define you
Believing others can anticipate your needs
Expecting others to fill your needs automatically
Falling apart so someone will take care of you
Assuming responsibility for others' feelings or behaviors

Difficulty forming and maintaining close relationships
Minimizing or denying true feelings

Signs of Healthy Boundaries

Having clear preferences and acting upon them
Recognizing how you feel
Trusting your own intuition while being open to others' opinions
Having personal standards that apply to everyone, demand accountability, and are flexible
Taking strong reactions to others' behaviors as information
Only doing favors you choose to do
Feeling mostly secure and clear
Remaining aware of your choices
Living a life that mostly approximates what you always wanted for yourself

Daring to set boundaries is about having the courage to love

ourselves
even when
we risk
disappointing
others.

-Brené Brown

Ponder This...

When are you most likely to set harsh or lenient boundaries?

_____

_____

_____

What helps you set healthy boundaries?

_____

_____

_____

Mark the examples of unhealthy and healthy boundaries above that resonate with you. What do you need in order to transform unhealthy boundaries into healthy ones?

_____

_____

_____

List at least three examples of healthy boundaries you need to set with drugs.

_____

_____

_____

Note To Loved Ones

Boundary setting might be the single most important thing you can do to support your loved one's recovery from addiction. By setting healthy boundaries for yourself, your loved one will learn that their relationship with drugs impacts those around them. Boundaries will also serve to keep you safe and capable of providing appropriate support. Check out _Get Your Loved One Sober_ for boundary-setting strategies and information.

Recommended Reading

Brown, C. B. (2012). *Daring Greatly: How the Courage to be Vulnerable Transforms the Way We Live, Love, Parent, and Lead.* New York, NY: Gotham.

Katherine, A. (2000.) *Where to Draw the Line?: How to Set Healthy Boundaries Every Day.* New York, NY: Fireside. (Author's note: This book contains language about addiction that is inconsistent with the approach used in this workbook. Nevertheless, it provides helpful information and exercises for improving boundaries throughout one's life.)

Chapter 8
Come As You Are

 "There is only one of you in all of time, this expression is unique. And if you block it, it will never exist through any other medium and it will be lost. The world will not have it. It is not your business to determine how good it is nor how valuable nor how it compares with other expressions. It is your business to keep it yours."

- Martha Graham

The relationship we have to ourselves is essential to our relationships with others, including drugs. One's relationship to self informs their lifestyle choices and ability to deal with life's challenges. The better we know ourselves, the more likely we are to succeed in life. We need to understand our own needs, wants, fears, and boundaries in order to navigate life effectively.

In order to know oneself, we must be radically accepting of our whole person. That means accepting both the good and the bad bits. This is where a self-compassion practice comes in handy. When we practice self-compassion we are able to have healthier reactions to our needs and fears.

Self-compassion is the act of radically accepting ourselves for all of our strengths and weaknesses. This practice is difficult for most of us, but particularly so if we come from toxic or traumatic histories.

The narratives we heard about ourselves growing up continue to impact and influence us into adulthood. The way you think your caregivers felt about you is likely the way you still feel about yourself. This can be good or it can create obstacles in your life.

If you internalized a sense of being bad, broken, or unlovable then you probably experience intense shame and self-criticism. Self-compassion can help you heal the wounds of childhood and provide an opportunity to reparent yourself.

Self-Compassion & Reparenting

Reparenting can be a helpful technique when cultivating self-compassion. It is the act of acknowledging your wounds and responding with compassion and nurture. For example, you may experience overwhelming anger when your partner forgets to unload the dishwasher. On the surface, you are able to recognize that your reaction is exaggerated, but you can't shake the intensity of the feeling. This likely means a trauma point has been hit.

Acknowledge that a part of you feels really hurt. Don't judge it. Just see it.

Get curious. What might this hurt part of yourself need in this moment? Perhaps just being seen is enough. Or maybe it wants comfort. Imagine a younger version of yourself. What does the younger version of yourself need to feel safe, comforted, nurtured?

- Curl up into a ball in bed
- Reach out to a compassionate friend
- Place your hand on your chest and take several deep, long breaths
- Take a walk and get some fresh air
- Give yourself permission to feel sad, hurt, scared
- Take time to rest in a comfortable space

Exercise: Identify Your Strengths

Identify something positive about yourself using each letter of the alphabet.

A _____

B _____

C _____

D _____

E _____

F _____

G _____

H _____

I _____

J _____

K _____

L _____

M _____

N _____

O _____

P _____

Q _____

R _____

S _____

T _____

U _____

V _____

W _____

X _____

Y _____

Z _____

Write about how you've used each of your strengths in the past.

_____

_____

_____

_____

_____

_____

_____

_____

_____

_____

_____

_____

_____

_____
_____
_____
_____
_____
_____
_____
_____
_____
_____

Write about the importance of each characteristic for you.

_____
_____
_____
_____
_____
_____
_____
_____
_____

_____

_____

_____

_____

_____

_____

_____

_____

_____

_____

_____

_____

_____

Self-Compassion Tribe

Self-compassion expert Lea Seigen Shinraku, MFT begins group meetings with this invocation to our sources of safety. Use this mindfulness exercise to access self-compassion resources when you feel shame or self-critical.

Find a comfortable place to sit for at least five minutes and up to 30 minutes. Make sure the place is safe as you might experience intense feelings during this exercise. You may choose to record yourself reading the words below and playing back the recording for yourself.

Close your eyes. Imagine yourself surrounded by warmth, love, and safety. Bring to mind the images, places, people, animals, and things that you associate with unconditional love. What you imagine may be real or imaginary. They may be a part of your personal history or something you've longed for. The images, places, people, and things you bring to mind will make up your self-compassion tribe.

Imagine a place where you feel sheltered in safety and love. What does this sanctuary look like? What are its features? What's the temperature like there? What does it smell like? Get as familiar with this place as possible, tuning into the different senses. Remember, it can be a real place or one you make up.

Bring to mind beings (people or animals) that you associate with protection, acceptance, and love. The people may have once played an important role in your life. Or maybe they're a character from a favorite book or movie. Perhaps there's an animal, real or mythical, that you identify with. Let yourself become overwhelmed with the presence of these beings.

What objects create feelings of refuge or love for you? Maybe you had a special toy to calm you down when you were a child. Or perhaps you recall a talisman from a favorite story. If nothing comes to mind, create an object of security or asylum for yourself.

Now bring to mind the members of your self-compassion tribe. Imagine yourself in your sanctuary surrounded by the people, animals, and objects that love and protect you unconditionally. Take a moment to acknowledge each member of your tribe. Notice what each member has to offer towards your self-compassion practice.

Before opening your eyes, imagine letting every cell in your body soak in all that has been offered by these beings and objects. Take a few moments to feel it in your hands, your feet, your belly, your chest.

Practice this exercise once a day while building your self-compassion practice. In a moment of shame or self-criticism call upon the resources of your self-compassion tribe. Practice kindness towards and acceptance of yourself.

Rewrite Your Story

Often, addiction becomes a part of a person's identity. Powerlessness over changing a behavior coupled with stigma about drug use can cause a person struggling with addiction to feel like a failure, a loser, or irreparably broken. Causing pain to others due to addiction can lead to beliefs like, *I'm no good, I only hurt people,* or *how can anyone ever love me?*

These feelings of shame and worthlessness can start to feel like inevitabilities if experienced repeatedly over a long period of time. And messages of "lazy, lying, thieving addicts" only reinforces these beliefs.

An important aspect of recovery will be reclaiming your identity as a person who uses drugs or as a person who formerly used drugs. Remember, this is only one facet of your identity. **There's so much more to you than your behavior.**

Exercise: Recover Your Identity

Write about how you currently see yourself and how you think others see you. Who are you as a person? What are the different parts of your identity that make you who you are today? Be sure to include the shadow parts — the aspects of yourself you wish were different or nonexistent.

_____

_____

_____

_____

_____

_____

_____

_____

_____

_____

_____

_____

_____

_____

_____

_____

_____

_____

_____

_____

there is no perfect narrative for recovery.
there is no perfect narrative for recovery.
there is no perfect narrative for recovery.
there is no perfect narrative for recovery.
there is no perfect narrative for recovery.
there is no perfect narrative for recovery.
there is no perfect narrative for recovery.
there is no perfect narrative for recovery.
there is no perfect narrative for recovery.
there is no perfect narrative for recovery.
there is no perfect narrative for recovery.

23/09/16
IG: FRIZZKIDART

Take several minutes to practice a self-compassion technique. Now, write a new narrative about yourself. Imagine who you can be as your best self. Remember, this includes those shadow parts, too. When looking through a self-compassionate lens, who are you as a person and how do others see you?

_____

_____

_____

_____

_____

_____

_____

_____

_____

_____

_____

_____

_____

_____

_____

_____

_____

_____

_____

_____

_____

_____

_____

Ponder This...

What's most challenging about practicing self-compassion?

_____

_____

_____

Using a self-compassionate lens, describe why you developed an unhealthy relationship to drugs.

_____

_____

_____

With this same lens, describe why relapse is a part of the change process.

_____

_____

_____

Sources

Loue, S. (2008). *The Transformative Power of Metaphor in Therapy*. New York, NY: Springer Publishing Company, LLC.

Shinraku, L. S. (2016). *Self-Compassion Tribe*. Used with author's permission. For more information visit http://www.sfcenterforselfcompassion.com

Recommended Reading

Neff, K. (2011). *Self-Compassion: The Proven Power of Being Kind to Yourself*. New York, NY: Harper Collins.

Brown, B. (2015). *Rising Strong: How the Ability to Reset Transforms the Way We Live, Love, Parent, and Lead*. New York, NY: Random House.

Chapter 9
Evaluating Your Relationship with Drugs

As you've learned throughout this workbook, we develop relationships to drugs because they offer us something. This chapter will aim to help you identify the relationship, personal, and lifestyle needs you meet by using drugs.

Let's start by examining the relationships you form with drugs. Imagine the relationship you have to drugs as a romantic relationship. If you use multiple drugs, you are likely to have different relationships to each one. Jot down the first few words that come to mind when you think about each drug. Don't overthink it! Let yourself free associate.

My Relationships to Drugs	
Drug	Relationship Characteristics
alcohol	
nicotine	
opioids	
cocaine	
amphetamine	
kratom	
cannabis	
synthetic cannabis	
ketamine	
nitrous oxide	
DXM	
GHB	
benzodiazepines	
MDMA	
MDA	
psilocybin	
LSD	
mescaline	
2CB	
DMT	
NBOMes	

Let's go a little deeper. Identify your attachment style to each drug, the needs met by using, and the values honored or violated by having a relationship with the drug.

More About My Relationships to Drugs			
Drug	Attachment Style	Needs Met	Values Honored and/or Violated
alcohol			
nicotine			
opioids			
cocaine			
amphetamine			
kratom			
cannabis			
synthetic cannabis			
ketamine			
nitrous oxide			
DXM			
GHB			
benzodiazepines			
MDMA			
MDA			
psilocybin			
LSD			
mescaline			
2CB			
DMT			
NBOMes			

Now let's focus only on the drug(s) to which you have a problematic relationship.

If the drug were a person, how would you describe them as a partner?

_____

_____

_____

What do you like about this partner?

_____

_____

_____

What don't you like?

_____

_____

_____

When is this partner there for you? How are they there for you?

_____

_____

_____

Before reading on, take a moment to practice a self-compassion exercise. Take a deep breath.

What does it mean that you continue to engage in a problematic relationship with this partner?

_____

_____

_____

What relationships from the past or present does this remind you of?

_____

_____

_____

Ponder This...

Gather all the data you have about your relationship to drugs. Review the decisional balance exercise from Chapter 2. Reflect on your free associations in the first exercise of this chapter. Identify the values that you honor or violate when using problematically. Identify the attachment style you have with drugs. Make a list of the feelings you have before, during, and after problematic use. Write about the boundaries you have with drugs.

My Boundaries with Drugs

Feelings Before, During, & After Problematic Use

Benefits & Costs of My Relationship to Drugs

My Attachment Styles to Drugs

Drug Relationship Characteristics

Values Honored & Violated

Paint a mental picture with this information. What do you see?

———

———

———

How has your relationship to drugs addressed the unmet needs in your relationships, career, health, and lifestyle?

———

———

———

———

———

———

Grieving

Changing the relationship you've formed with drugs requires a grieving process. Whether you choose abstinence or moderation, the relationship you are forming is new — meaning the old relationship will end. Although this may seem like a welcome relief on the surface, there are likely feelings of pain or fear about changing how you interact with your drug of choice. Remember, you've depended on your relationship to drugs for escape, comfort, and coping. You are choosing to leave behind something that feels familiar and dependable.

> "In grief, just like in death, there is a transformation for the living."
>
> -Elizabeth Kübler-Ross

Grief expert Elizabeth Kübler-Ross said there are two important reasons to grieve a loss:

"First, those who grieve well, live well. Second, and most important, grief is the healing process of the heart, soul, and mind; it is the path that returns us to wholeness. It shouldn't be a matter of *if* you will grieve, the question is *when* will you grieve. And until we do, we suffer from the effects of that unfinished business."

Stages of Grief

Grief is a lot like change: it's a nonlinear and incremental process. You may notice some parallels between the stages of grief and the stages of change.

Denial

At the onset of a loss, one experiences shock. Disbelief, confusion, and denial are common experiences. Life seems meaningless and empty. One feels lost and numb.

- *This can't be happening!*
- *I don't feel anything.*
- *Life makes no sense.*
- *I don't need to change my relationship with drugs. I've got this under control.*

What does denial sound like for you?

_____

_____

_____

Anger

Anger is a healthy part of grief in that it gives the process some structure. You are probably very familiar with anger and have strategies for managing it. Underneath the anger there are feelings of pain that will surface later in the process, but for now anger gives you strength and energy.

- *Why is this happening to me?*
- *This isn't fair.*
- *How could I have done this to myself for so long?*
- *Why can't I be a normal drinker?*
- *No one understands me.*

What does anger sound like for you?

_____

_____

_____

Bargaining

In an attempt to avoid the pain of grief, one will find themselves bargaining. This stage is riddled with "if only" and "what if" statements and is often accompanied by guilt.

- *If only I had a better job, then my relationship to alcohol would be healthy.*

- *I don't want to go to therapy. What if I only use with friends?*
- *If only I could go back in time and never have started using.*
- *If only I had started treatment earlier, I wouldn't have hurt my family.*

What does bargaining sound like for you?

_____

_____

_____

Depression

At last, the real pain of grief and loss has arrived. Those around you may not tolerate this stage well and encourage you to "snap out of it" or "move on." The sadness, despair, and hopelessness you feel is a normal and healthy reaction to loss. You formed a deep relationship to drugs in order to cope and the choice to end that relationship is scary, challenging, and painful.

- *Why should I go on?*
- *This sucks.*
- *I feel so empty.*
- *This sadness feels endless.*
- *This is so hard!*

What does depression sound like for you?

_____

_____

_____

Acceptance

Once you have given the grief process time and space to unfold, you will arrive at acceptance. This doesn't mean you've "gotten over it" or "moved on," it simply means that you are fully present with reality. You accept that you must create a different relationship to drugs. You accept that you will have to make changes in your lifestyle and personal relationships. You commit to making choices that are in line with your values. You experience growth and healing.

- *I want to find comfort in other activities besides using.*
- *I'm going to work on my relationships so I can depend on others in times of need.*
- *I need to address my mental health issues.*
- *I feel empowered about my choices.*
- *I'm not able to use in a responsible way. I need to abstain.*

What does acceptance sound like for you?

_____

_____

_____

Ponder This...

Which stage of grief are you currently in?

_____

_____

_____

How do the stages of grief compare to the stages of change?

_____

_____

_____

Think about other times you've grieved a loss. What helped you cope with it? What are some values-based choices you can make to help you cope with grief today?

_____

_____

_____

Sources
Kübler-Ross, E. & Kessler, D. (2005). *On Grief and Grieving.* New York, NY: Scribner.

Recommended Reading
Denning, P. & Little, J. (2017). *Over the Influence* (2nd ed.). New York, NY: The Guilford Press.

Chapter 10
Accepting Your Emotions

Our minds and bodies may not come with a user's manual, but we do have a built-in notification system. Emotions sound an alarm that clue us in on internal states and external situations.

Robert Plutchik, a psychologist who studied emotions, regarded them as bioevolutionary triggers of behavior that have high survival value for a species. For example, the flight or fight response is triggered by fear and procreation is triggered by love. He identified eight primary, opposing emotions:

joy vs sadness
trust vs disgust
fear vs anger
surprise vs anticipation

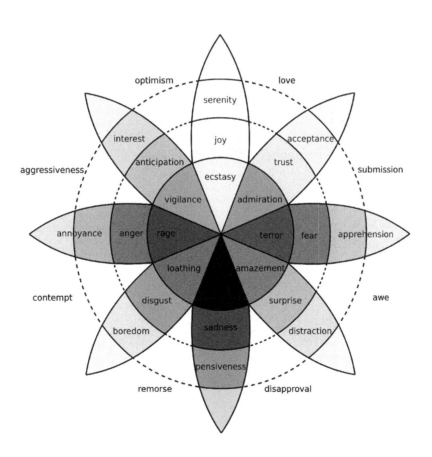

Image by Machine Elf 1735

These basic emotions mix with one another and have different intensities, like colors. Bring to mind a favorite painting. Think of all the different colors mixing and dancing around on the canvas. The colors in the painting may be distinct from one another or they might overlap, one drowning out the other.

Your emotional self is like a painting. Emotions mix and dance around in our minds and bodies; rarely do we experience one emotion at a time. And sometimes one emotion acts as a mask for a deeper more vulnerable one, such as when anger masks powerlessness. Here are some examples of complex emotions:

love = joy + trust
contempt = disgust + anger
submission = trust + fear
optimism = anticipation + joy
remorse = sadness + disgust

These feeling states help us identify what drives our thoughts and behaviors. Emotions can clue us in about unconscious desires and fears or opportunities and dangers in our environment.

Like paint, emotions are fluid. They ebb, flow, rise, fall, twist, and turn, but they are never constant. This is why trying to hold on to a particular emotional state or trying to create one doesn't work very well. This fact is especially helpful to remember when you're in an unpleasant emotional state. Think of the emotion as a wave. As it's rising, it may feel like it's going to crush you, but you're a better surfer than you let yourself think! Eventually the wave will mellow out and settle down on the shore.

Ponder This...

Why do you think we experience emotions? What's helpful about them? What's challenging about them?

_____

_____

_____

Which emotions color your canvas most days?

_____

_____

_____

Look at the emotions wheel. Which emotions do you never or rarely experience?

_____

_____

_____

What do you think your emotions are telling you about unconscious desires or fears?

_____

_____

_____

Write about a time when an emotion helped you navigate a difficult situation?

_____

_____

_____

How long do your emotion "waves" last? Are they longer or shorter for unpleasant emotions?

_____

_____

_____

Think of your current coping strategies for managing emotions. Do you have enough? How confident do you feel using them? Do you know how to anticipate which strategies will be most helpful?

_____

_____

_____

Learning to Surf

Learning to surf the wave of emotion becomes particularly helpful when we experience painful emotions. Of course we would rather avoid feelings of pain, but just like physical pain we can learn a lot from getting hurt.

Physical pain gives us feedback about potentially dangerous stimuli. If you touch a hot pan, the nerves in your hand send a signal to your brain to pull away. It is important to consider painful emotions in the same manner.

Emotional pain, whether it be sadness, fear, anger, grief, or powerlessness, gives us important information about the world and people around us. Understanding your painful emotions will empower you to make better decisions in your life and relationships.

> "The pain now is part of the happiness then. That's the deal."
> -C.S. Lewis

If you always feel hurt after interacting with your co-worker, this may signal the need for different boundaries with them.

If you feel overwhelming rage when your partner is unable to meet your needs, there may be more to learn about past traumas.

One of the most important tools in your recovery toolkit is embracing and surfing painful emotions. Now, mastering this will never make pain disappear or stop from showing up. Pain will never feel good, but it will become increasingly tolerable. As you get better at accepting and navigating pain you will feel more empowered, confident, and trusting of yourself.

In order to achieve radical acceptance of painful emotions you will need to practice curiosity with your emotions, self-compassion, mindfulness, and surfing.

Exercise: Get to Know Your Pain

The sooner you accept that pain is a normal part of human life, the better you will become at navigating it. The next time you feel a painful emotion, take the time to get to know it. Use mindfulness to engage your observer mind. Curiosity is another powerful tool that can help you navigate your emotions instead of feeling overwhelmed by them. Ask yourself, "What about my situation is causing me to feel these emotions?"

Notice and name the emotional pain you are feeling. You may be aware of multiple emotions at once. Name as many as you're aware of.

Rate the pain on a scale from one to ten, one being uncomfortable and ten being extreme anguish or despair.

If the pain registers at five or below continue with the exercise. If it registers above six, practice exercises from the mindfulness chapter until the pain decreases to a manageable level.

Notice where you feel the painful emotion in your body.

Notice how the pain influences your thinking.

Allow images, colors, and stories influenced by the pain to enter your mind.

If it starts to become too overwhelming, stop and practice diaphragmatic breathing until the pain returns to a manageable level.

Once the pain has subsided, log it below and write about your experience or share it with someone you trust.

Pain Log		
Date	**Unpleasant emotion(s)**	**Intensity** **(1=uncomfortable, 10=anguish)**
		1 2 3 4 5 6 7 8 9 10
	Bodily Sensations	**Thoughts during Pain**
Date	**Unpleasant emotion(s)**	**Intensity** **(1=uncomfortable, 10=anguish)**
		1 2 3 4 5 6 7 8 9 10
	Bodily Sensations	**Thoughts during Pain**
Date	**Unpleasant emotion(s)**	**Intensity** **(1=uncomfortable, 10=anguish)**
		1 2 3 4 5 6 7 8 9 10
	Bodily Sensations	**Thoughts during Pain**

Date	Unpleasant emotion(s)	Intensity (1=uncomfortable, 10=anguish)
		1 2 3 4 5 6 7 8 9 10
	Bodily Sensations	Thoughts during Pain

Date	Unpleasant emotion(s)	Intensity (1=uncomfortable, 10=anguish)
		1 2 3 4 5 6 7 8 9 10
	Bodily Sensations	Thoughts during Pain

Date	Unpleasant emotion(s)	Intensity (1=uncomfortable, 10=anguish)
		1 2 3 4 5 6 7 8 9 10
	Bodily Sensations	Thoughts during Pain

Date	Unpleasant emotion(s)	Intensity (1=uncomfortable, 10=anguish)
		1 2 3 4 5 6 7 8 9 10
	Bodily Sensations	Thoughts during Pain

Recommended Reading

Harris, R. (2008). *The Happiness Trap: How to Stop Struggling and Start Living*. Boulder, CO: Trumpeter Books.

Chapter 11
Managing Anger

Anger is an important and valuable emotion. It protects us from perceived threats and empowers us to take action when we perceive injustice. Sometimes our minds are too sensitive and falsely perceive threat or injustice when it doesn't exist.

Oftentimes people who struggle with addiction have a complicated relationship with anger. They may use drugs problematically in order to mask feelings of anger or to lessen intense anger, like rage.

Because anger is such an effective shield from harm, it often shows up when more tender emotions like sadness, grief, powerlessness, or fear are present. This presentation can be adaptive when there is no chance for the tender emotion to be expressed, such as during an argument with someone who becomes physically violent or during a mugging. Anger is warranted and adaptive in those situations. But short of being assaulted or in physical danger, it is usually better to communicate from our tender places than from our anger.

To be clear, this doesn't mean that we shouldn't express feelings of anger towards loved ones or in situations where injustice has occurred. The point here is that when you're feeling angry, there's more going on beneath the surface. Healthy expressions of anger can be achieved through nonviolent communication. Healthy expressions of anger never include hitting or name calling.

Think of anger as an umbrella emotion. It shows up to shield you from getting hurt. Unfortunately, its effects are more like an overprotective parent than a deflecting shield. **In order to grow, we sometimes have to face life's challenges head on.**

The next time you feel angry, practice curiosity and try to identify the other feelings underneath the umbrella.

If you struggle with controlling your anger, first you will want to practice mindfulness and grounding exercises.

Anger can cause us to respond impulsively. This usually ends up causing more harm than protection. The shield becomes a bulldozer destroying everything in its path. This isn't very adaptive at all.

The key to anger management is to become aware of its earliest stirrings. It may seem like you go from 0 to 60 in one second, but once you practice mindfulness you will learn that you start to become activated well before you blow up. If fact, the secret to managing any emotion is getting good at identifying it in its early stages.

Don't let smaller emotions like frustration, annoyance, irritability, or discomfort build up to anger or explosive rage. When you notice an unpleasant emotion name it, rate it, and de-escalate it.

Anger Management

Name the unpleasant emotions you are feeling. There are probably several emotions present, see if you can name more than one.

Rate the intensity of the emotion on a scale from one to ten. One is slight discomfort and ten is extreme rage that could lead to physical violence.

Use diaphragmatic breathing to de-escalate the intensity of the emotion. Remember, you cannot make emotions disappear but you can manage them.

Once the emotion is at a tolerable level, evaluate your basic needs.

Are you hungry? Lonely? Tired?

Take care of your basic needs first. If you are still feeling upset, continue practicing curiosity and let the painful emotions underneath the anger inform your actions. You may need to take an action that changes your circumstances, such as setting a boundary or making a request.

When you choose to express your anger, make sure you are practicing assertiveness and nonviolent communication. It is never ok to intentionally hurt another person with your words or through violent acts. You have better tools now for getting your point across and influencing others.

Exercise: Anger Tracking

The more you learn about what triggers anger, the better you will be at de-escalating it. Keep a log of every time you feel angry. Note how angry you felt. Rate the anger a "1" if you felt annoyed, "2" if you felt angry, and "3" if you felt rage. Next, log what made you angry and how you responded. Finally, consider whether you could have responded differently and what a better response would have been.

Anger Log		
Date	Trigger	Intensity
		1—annoyed 2—angry 3—enraged

	Actual Response	Better Response

Date	Trigger	Intensity
		1—annoyed 2—angry 3—enraged

	Actual Response	Better Response

Date	Trigger	Intensity
		1—annoyed 2—angry 3—enraged

	Actual Response	Better Response

Date	Trigger	Intensity
		1—annoyed 2—angry 3—enraged

	Actual Response	Better Response

Date	Trigger	Intensity
		1—annoyed 2—angry 3—enraged

	Actual Response	Better Response

Date	Trigger	Intensity
		1—annoyed 2—angry 3—enraged

	Actual Response	Better Response

Date	Trigger	Intensity
		1—annoyed 2—angry 3—enraged
	Actual Response	Better Response

Date	Trigger	Intensity
		1—annoyed 2—angry 3—enraged
	Actual Response	Better Response

Date	Trigger	Intensity
		1—annoyed 2—angry 3—enraged
	Actual Response	Better Response

Date	Trigger	Intensity
		1—annoyed 2—angry 3—enraged
	Actual Response	Better Response

Chapter 12
Managing Stress

"We will be more successful in all our endeavors if we can let go of the habit of running all the time, and take little pauses to relax and recenter ourselves. And we'll also have a lot more joy in living. "

– Thich Nhat Hanh

Stress is a normal part of human life and while we can't avoid it, there are many things we can do to manage it. Stress can be adaptive or debilitating. It can motivate us to meet our goals or paralyze us with feelings of overwhelm. By managing stress levels, we can use it to our advantage.

When unmanaged, stress is often a trigger for problematic drug use. **By assessing and reducing the amount of stress in your life, you can decrease chaotic use.**

First, let's determine how much stress there currently is in your life. Read the signs of too much stress below and circle the ones that apply to you. These symptoms aren't always caused by stress. It may be worth speaking with your doctor about your symptoms to rule out underlying medical conditions that need treatment.

Signs of Excessive Stress

Physical symptoms
- Extended fatigue
- Dry mouth
- Weight loss or gain
- Excessive sweating
- Frequent illness
- Gastrointestinal problems
- Grinding of teeth
- Headaches
- High blood pressure

- Pounding heart
- Stiff neck or aching lower back

Emotional symptoms

- Anger
- Anxiety or edginess
- Depression
- Fatigue
- Hypervigilance
- Impulsiveness
- Increased criticism, disenchantment, or cynicism
- Inability to concentrate
- Irritability
- Trouble remembering things

Behavioral symptoms

- Absenteeism or tardiness
- Crying
- Unwillingness to take vacation
- Changes in appetite
- Sleep disturbances
- Reduced physical activity
- Increased drug use
- Problems communicating
- Sexual problems
- Social isolation

In order to reduce stress, you will need to identify the areas of your life that contribute towards it. Once you know what's adding to your stress, you can implement strategies to eliminate or reduce the sources. Circle the ones that apply to you.

Daily Sources of Stress

- Disliking daily activities
- Lack of privacy
- Dissatisfaction with work
- Ethnic or racial conflict
- Conflicts with loved ones
- Being let down by friends
- Conflict with supervisor at work
- Social rejection
- Too many things to do at once
- Being taken for granted
- Financial conflicts with loved ones
- Having trust betrayed

- Separation from loved ones
- Having contributions overlooked
- Struggling to meet your own standards of performance and accomplishment
- Being taken advantage of
- Not enough leisure time
- Having actions misunderstood
- Cash-flow difficulties
- Having too many responsibilities
- Not enough time to meet obligations
- Financial burdens
- High levels of noise
- Social isolation
- Being ignored
- Dissatisfaction with physical appearance
- Unsatisfactory housing conditions
- Transportation problems
- Procrastination
- Not enough time alone
- Overwhelm from watching the news
- Distress about politics
- Distress over social media interactions

Exercise: Stress log

Similar to the anger log that you kept, track incidents of stress for at least one week, but preferably for a month. Note the situation that resulted in stress. Rate the intensity from slightly stressful to very stressful. At the end of the tracking period, look over your log and identify the areas where you can eliminate stress.

Stress Log		
Date	Trigger	Intensity
		slightly stressful | stressful | very stressful
	How can I eliminate or reduce this stressor?	

Date	Trigger	Intensity
		slightly stressful | stressful | very stressful
	How can I eliminate or reduce this stressor?	

Date	Trigger	Intensity
		slightly stressful | stressful | very stressful
	How can I eliminate or reduce this stressor?	

Date	Trigger	Intensity
		slightly stressful | stressful | very stressful
	How can I eliminate or reduce this stressor?	

Date	Trigger	Intensity
		slightly stressful | stressful | very stressful
	How can I eliminate or reduce this stressor?	

Date	Trigger	Intensity
		slightly stressful | stressful | very stressful
	How can I eliminate or reduce this stressor?	

Date	Trigger	Intensity
		slightly stressful | stressful | very stressful
	How can I eliminate or reduce this stressor?	

You may have to come up with creative solutions for decreasing stress in your life. You may decide to delegate tasks to others. You may have to sacrifice behaviors that feel like control or power. You may need to give up some of your time. You may need to spend more money.

Here are some examples of choices you can make to eliminate some stress in your life:

- Let family members take over some of the household chores. You may have to sacrifice having things done exactly the way you like them.
- Ask for help from co-workers with tasks that seem daunting, overwhelming, or unfamiliar.
- Enlist support from your community. Start a carpooling group, schedule play dates, start a monthly rotating dinner party with friends.
- Start saying no. Be honest with yourself about your availability before agreeing to something. Do you really have time? Do you have the emotional bandwidth?
- If you have the means, pay for services that decrease the amount of tasks you need to complete. Hire a housecleaner or landscaper. Have your groceries and household supplies delivered.
- If your job is a source of chronic, overwhelming stress consider looking for another one.
- If your relationship is a source of chronic, overwhelming stress consider counseling.
- Spend time with people who support and validate you. Limit time with people who exhaust or demean you.
- Make a budget to decrease stress about money and to live within your means. You may have to sacrifice luxuries, but you'll feel a whole lot better.
- Start a savings plan. You'll feel great after meeting your financial goal.
- Observe your thoughts while feeling stressed. Do the stories in your mind make the stress worse? Are you making assumptions, jumping to conclusions, predicting the future? Is the

negative filter of your mind on? Adjust your thinking to reflect reality as much as possible and stop travelling to the past or future.

- Practice acceptance. Stress will always be a part of your life. Remind yourself that it can be used to your advantage and motivate you to meet a goal.

Chapter 13
Overcoming Shame

Shame is a hallmark of addiction. When behavior falls outside of our value system, hurts others, or causes problems in our lives a breeding ground for shame is born.

Shame is often times confused for guilt, so let's clarify the difference. Guilt occurs when we feel badly about an action we have or haven't taken. We recognize a mistake has been made and we feel badly about it. Shame can be much more intense than that. It isn't focused on our actions, but rather on our worth as a person.

Shame occurs when we perceive ourselves as a bad person and this emotional state can cause paralysis. If I'm a bad person, then I'm destined to do bad things, hurt others, and hurt myself. Shame is all-encompassing. It not only colors your self-perception but also the perception of your actions, relationships, and worth in the world.

People with addiction experience a higher degree of shame than others. This is partly due to the damage addiction can have on a person's life. Addiction can drive a person to engage in behaviors that are harmful to themselves and others, leading to feelings of guilt and shame. But shame is also induced by the countless stigmatized images and stories of addiction present in modern culture. Even the word "addict" can elicit feelings of shame because of the negative context in which it is so often used. People with addiction are depicted as untrustworthy, violent, thieves, criminals, traitors, and downright awful people. Although it is true that humans do behave in these ways, it is not exclusive to people with addiction.

Overcoming shame is an essential part of developing healthy relationships to drugs. The same practices used to manage other difficult emotions can be applied to shame.

Practice mindfulness to observe when you experience shame, how it feels in your body, and how it influences your thoughts.

Part of what makes shame especially challenging to deconstruct is that we've been fed shame-based messages since childhood. Think about all the things you were told you shouldn't do, all the behaviors you were punished or reprimanded for, and all the negative messages you got about who you are.

Society loves to create rules about how we should look, who we should love, what sex is supposed to look like, how relationships should be structured, and the definition of success.

Ponder This...

What are some of the rules or messages you've received about how to live your life?

_____

_____

_____

How have these messages resulted in feelings of shame?

_____

_____

_____

Have you ever felt like a bad person because of your gender, race, economic status, sexual orientation, or disability? Write examples of these shame-based thoughts below.

_____

_____

_____

Write examples of shame-based thoughts related to your relationship with drugs below.

_____

_____

_____

Exercise: Combat Shame-Based Thinking

Remember that shame's function is to beat you down. Practice reality testing with shame-based thoughts. For every self-criticism have a self-compassion statement.

Make a list of the shame-based or self-critical thoughts you experience when feeling shame. In the column on the right write a counter argument. Conjure the best defense attorney you can imagine here. Remember that you have worth, value, and lovability just as you are and just because you are. You don't need to work for those attributes. They were given to you at birth.

From Self-Loathing to Self-Love	
Self-Critical Thinking	Self-Compassionate Counter

<table>
<tr><td></td><td></td></tr>
<tr><td></td><td></td></tr>
<tr><td></td><td></td></tr>
<tr><td></td><td></td></tr>
<tr><td></td><td></td></tr>
</table>

Exercise: Loving Kindness Meditation

Loving kindness or *metta* is a meditation practice used for moving through feelings of shame, guilt, or blame. You can also practice it when feeling angry, resentful, or judgmental towards others. Consider recording this script and playing it back to yourself.

Sit in a comfortable position so that you are sitting relaxed with a straight back and relaxed shoulders. Allow your hands to rest in your lap. Close your eyes.

Settle into an awareness of your body. Now become aware of your breath. Feel into your body right now and notice what's there. Be open to whatever you're experiencing in your body in this moment. Connect to your breath and notice the wave-like movement in your belly.

In this practice, you'll be cultivating loving kindness. We all have within us a natural capacity for loving kindness; friendship that is unconditional, open, gentle, and supportive. Loving kindness is a natural opening of a compassionate heart towards ourselves and others. It's a wish for everyone to be happy.

Begin to develop loving kindness towards yourself by allowing your heart to open with tenderness. Allow yourself to remember and open up to your basic goodness. You might remember times you've been kind or generous. Or perhaps you recall your natural desire to be happy and free of suffering.

If acknowledging your own goodness is difficult, look at yourself through the eyes of someone who loves you. What does that person love about you? Or maybe you recall the unconditional love you felt from a beloved pet.

It may help to picture yourself as a young child, perhaps four or five years old, if that allows tender feelings of kindness to flow more easily.

As you experience this love notice how it feels in your body. Maybe you feel some warmth, heat in the face, a smile, or a sense of expansiveness. This is loving kindness, a natural feeling that is always accessible to all of us. Rest with this feeling of open, unconditional love for a few minutes.

Let yourself bask in the energy of loving kindness: breathing it in, breathing it out, inviting feelings of peace and acceptance.

Now, begin to wish yourself well by extending words of loving kindness to yourself:

May I be filled with loving kindness.
May I be held in loving kindness.
May I feel connected and calm.
May I accept myself just as I am.
May I be happy.
May I know the natural joy of being alive.

Repeat these words of friendship and kindness to yourself once again:

May I be filled with loving kindness.
May I be held in loving kindness.
May I feel connected and calm.
May I accept myself just as I am.
May I be happy.
May I know the natural joy of being alive.

You can choose to stop here or keep going by extending the practice of loving kindness to others. Below is the continuation of the script for a full loving kindness practice.

Now, you can open the circle of loving kindness by bringing to mind someone dear to you. Someone you care about and who has always been supportive. Reflect on this person's basic goodness, sensing what in particular you love about them. In your heart, feel appreciation for this loved one and begin your offering:

May you be filled with loving kindness.
May you be held in loving kindness.
May you feel connected and calm.
May you accept yourself just as you are.
May you be happy.
May you know the natural joy of being alive.

Now bring to mind a neutral person. This is someone you might regularly see but don't know well. It might be a neighbor or grocery store clerk. Bring this person to mind now and repeat the words of loving kindness:

May you be filled with loving kindness.
May you be held in loving kindness.
May you feel connected and calm.
May you accept yourself just as you are.
May you be happy.
May you know the natural joy of being alive.

And now, if it's possible, bring to mind someone with whom you've had a difficult relationship. Perhaps it's someone you don't like to feel sympathy or compassion for. See if it's possible to let go of feelings of resentment or dislike for this person. Remind yourself to see this person as a whole being deserving of love and kindness, as someone who feels pain and anxiety, as someone who also suffers.

See if it's possible to extend to this person the words of loving kindness in your mind:

May you be filled with loving kindness.
May you be held in loving kindness.
May you feel connected and calm.
May you accept yourself just as you are.
May you be happy.
May you know the natural joy of being alive.

Now, allow your awareness to open out in all directions (yourself, a loved one, a neutral person, and a difficult person) and to all beings (humans and animals living everywhere, living in richness, poverty, war, hunger, abundance). Be aware of all the joys and sorrows that all beings experience.

May all beings be filled with loving kindness.
May all beings be held in loving kindness.
May all beings feel connected and calm.
May all beings accept themselves just as they are.
May all beings be happy.
May all beings know the natural joy of being alive.

And now, bring this practice to a close by coming back to extend kindness to yourself. Sit for awhile and bask in the energy of loving kindness you have generated here.

Recommended Reading
Bradshaw, J. (2005). *Healing the Shame that Binds You*. Deerfield Beach, FL: Health Communications.

Chapter 14
Managing Urges

"At the end of the day, we can endure much more than we think we can."

-Frida Kahlo

This is where the rubber meets the road. Managing urges is the most active part of preventing relapse and developing healthier relationships to drugs.

Harm reduction psychologist Dr. Andrew Tatarsky describes urges as the biological, psychological, and social aspects of addiction coming together. During an urge your brain is craving the chemical hit from the drug. Psychologically, you are thrust into a state of despair, discomfort, or panic. The social context informs which of your needs are or aren't being met. Are you feeling alone and craving connection? Are you at a party where others are having a good time with drugs?

An urge is typically experienced as an intense physical response. It may feel like the beginning of the addictive cycle, but as you'll learn momentarily there are quite a few things that happen beforehand. When first learning about your relationship to drugs, the urge is usually the most identifiable step in the cycle.

Urges themselves are not unhealthy. Humans experience urges for all kinds of things. Even when you crave something harmful, the need underlying the urge is healthy.

It will be necessary for you to resist urges in order to understand the unmet needs underlying your addiction.

Once you understand what the urge means, you may still choose to use. That's fine. The point here is to make informed decisions that align with your values.

First you'll need to identify the urge. Most people experience an increasing sense of tension, pressure, discomfort, or anxiety. Most likely this will occur in the area of your chest or abdomen. You may notice these sensations paired with intrusive thoughts, sometimes about using but not always.

Once you've identified an urge to use, you will need to learn how to surf it. That intense discomfort you feel will pass. You will likely experience it as a wave, growing in intensity over time but eventually crashing onto shore. Your job is to ride that wave without giving in to the urge. Good thing you've been practicing surfing with unpleasant emotions!

Urge surfing is hard work, so be patient and kind with yourself. Sometimes urges only last a few minutes while seeming endless at other times. Trust yourself while surfing. If it feels like the wave is too big, engage in an alternative quick fix. We'll look at what those are for you in a moment.

Before surfing, mentally prepare yourself for a challenge. Give yourself a pep talk.

While surfing, remember to breathe. Breathing will engage your parasympathetic nervous system and help you remain in control. Take big, deep breaths into your belly. Inhale for a count of 5, hold your breath for a count of 2, and exhale for a count of 10. Repeat this as many times as necessary while surfing. You may find yourself breathing this way for 5, 10, or 20 minutes. Do what you need to do to get through it. The best thing about this strategy is you can do it anytime, anywhere. You always have access to your breath.

Exercise: Urge Tracking

Use the chart below to track when you have urges. Tracking urges will help you start making connections to triggers and unmet needs. It also gives you feedback about how often you are experiencing urges and how intense they are. With the help of your therapist, you can use this data to make a robust responsible drug use or relapse prevention plan.

Urge Tracking					
Date	How long did it last?	What triggered it?	How intense was it?		
			mild	moderate	severe
			mild	moderate	severe
			mild	moderate	severe
			mild	moderate	severe
			mild	moderate	severe
			mild	moderate	severe
			mild	moderate	severe
			mild	moderate	severe
			mild	moderate	severe
			mild	moderate	severe

The Cycle

Now that you know what to do when experiencing an urge, let's try to understand the cycle leading up to it. The earlier you can catch yourself in the process, the easier is it to prevent relapse. This cycle is adapted from *Taking Back What's Been Stolen* by Elizabeth Corsale, MFT and Samantha Smithstein, PsyD.

Think of this cycle as the roadmap to relapse. Each step in the cycle offers a detour. But you have to realize where you are in order to make a turn.

Trigger

Keeping with the map analogy, this is your current location. The trigger could literally be your environment but it could also be your internal state of being. The trigger can be a place, person, object, thought, feeling, memory, or physical sensation. It can have a positive or negative connotation.

- Are you someplace where you've used before? Are you at your parents' house? Are you at a party?

- Did your ex just reach out to you again? Are you about to have a conversation with your sister? Did you pass someone on the street who reminded you of a dangerous person?
- Did you find your old paraphernalia while cleaning out the closet? Did you spot a child playing with a toy from your childhood? Did you see an item that you've been wanting for a long time?
- Are you stressing out about a presentation at work? Are you thinking about the current political situation? Are you beating yourself up over a mistake? Are you reminiscing about an injustice you experienced? Are you fantasizing about an escape?
- Are you feeling tired, alone, scared, sad, powerless, angry, overwhelmed, excited, happy, horny, celebratory, energized?
- Are you recalling how awful it felt the last time you were depressed? Are you remembering how amazing it felt the last you used? Are you reliving painful or pleasant memories?
- Are you in physical pain or discomfort? Have you experienced recent relief, comfort, or pleasure?

Craving

After encountering the trigger, your mind begins to crave something different. If the trigger has a negative connotation, you may crave escape or relief from the stressor. If the trigger is positive, you may crave fulfillment of something pleasurable. You can identify the craving by watching or listening to your thoughts. Write down your thoughts as you have them.

Fantasy

Now that you're craving something different, you begin to tell yourself a story about how the forthcoming events will play out. Or there may be a movie that plays out in your imagination about your current state.

Let's say you've been feeling stressed out due to work. You just got an email from your boss pushing your deadline up by a week. The email is the trigger. You begin craving escape from your work situation. You find yourself thinking about that beach in Baja where you went on vacation a couple of years ago. You reminisce about the sand, the color of the water, the margaritas. This is your fantasy.

A narrative is playing out in your mind related to what you were previously craving. Now, the fantasy is not always pleasant — you may have a distressing fantasy. The email from your boss may have triggered a craving to get him off your back. You may begin to think about what it would take to finish this project a week early. You may imagine missing a few important tasks and getting a negative review from your boss. A series of imagined scenes might play out from here: losing your job, being unable to find another one, blowing through your savings, and ending up at your parents' house unemployed and depressed.

Urge

At this point, your mind is pretty worked up. A stressor has triggered a craving and fantasy response. And even though you've only been fantasizing about how to gain relief or fulfillment, your brain can't tell the difference between fantasy and reality and is now anticipating a hit of dopamine. And the brain is very demanding! If it anticipates a reward but doesn't get it, it goes into freakout mode. The amygdala puts out a distress call. You experience this as a physiological response, an increasing sense of tension in your body.

Distorted Thinking

Not only are you worked up and uncomfortable at this point, but now you've really got to do something about it. After all, you're in a state of distress! Your neurons are firing rapidly to determine your best and most accessible course of action. And since the brain thrives on patterns, your brain is likely to get you to repeat a common or familiar course of action.

Your mind will now work all kinds of tricks to convince you to engage in a potentially problematic behavior and reality will become distorted in a number of ways. The stressor will appear increasingly unbearable, the relief increasingly attainable. And your drug of choice? It will appear as the only sensible, logical, and effective solution. Nothing else will work.

Distorted thinking will minimize the impact of your choice, exaggerate the intensity of the stressor, justify acting outside of your value system, and rationalize your decision to use. Be prepared to catch yourself in the act of distorting reality. Think about how you've done this in the past and write those thoughts down. You're more likely to catch distorted thinking if you know what to look for.

Planning & Seemingly Unimportant Decisions

You've convinced yourself to take action at this point, so now you're getting ready to make it happen. If the planning is conscious, you're plotting to acquire the drug and thinking about when you'll use it.

If it's unconscious, you're making a series of seemingly unimportant decisions that set you up for relapse.
- You skip lunch, leaving you with less energy to surf the urge.
- You exhaust yourself with work and when you get home you're even more stressed out.
- You tell yourself you don't need any support and can tackle this without reaching out to friends or your therapist.
- You decide to reach out to a friend for support. But in the back of your mind you know this friend enjoys the same drug you are trying to have a different relationship with. It is likely that this friend will suggest using as a solution to your problems.
- You decide that what you need is a long walk. But the route you've chosen takes you by three liquor stores.

Think about the seemingly harmless decisions you've made in the past that set you up to use problematically and write them down.

High Risk Situation

You are moments away from relapse now. This is the hardest point from which to take a detour. For some, the high risk situation occurs just before using. You are preparing the drug or it is in front of you ready to use. But for others, the high risk situation happens even before they have the drug at their disposal.

As you develop a healthier relationship to drugs, the high risk situation will change. For now, it might be that just having a difficult or painful experience makes it challenging to make a choice other than using. The high risk situation might be experiencing a specific emotion like anger or interacting with a specific person. It could be a specific place, time, or occasion. Maybe your relationship to drugs only becomes problematic on the weekends, at weddings, or when you go home for the holidays.

Track the situations when it's hardest to maintain a healthy relationship with drugs. Sometimes avoiding these situations will seem like the best strategy — and sometimes it is. But it is also important to develop a different moderation or abstinence plan for these situations.

Evaluation

After using, you tell yourself a story about what happened. If you've had a problematic experience you may feel shame, worthless, and failure. You might blame yourself or others. You may feel hopeless about your chances at having a different relationship with drugs.

Now is the time to pull out those self-compassion resources. Yes, you've made a decision you don't feel good about. Recall the underlying need that got the cycle started. **You deserve to have that need met.** You did the best you could with the resources you had at your disposal this time. Next time you can make a different decision.

Think about why it's important to make a different choice in the future. Remind yourself that relapse is an opportunity to learn about your relationship with drugs. Take this opportunity to identify the steps of the cycle, as they are fresh in your mind.

Exercise: Relapse Reflection Sheet

Which self-compassion strategies can I practice right now?

_____

_____

What was the underlying unmet need that got the cycle started?

_____

_____

Why is that need important?

_____

_____

_____

Why is it important to make a different choice next time I have an urge to use?

_____

_____

_____

Which values do I violate when I use drugs problematically?

_____

_____

_____

Which values do I honor when I resist urges to use?

_____

_____

_____

Fill out the cycle.

Trigger	
Craving	
Fantasy	

Urge	
Distorted Thinking	
Planning	
High Risk Situation	
Evaluation	

Where did I miss opportunities to take a detour?

_____

_____

_____

What choices do I want to make differently next time?

_____

_____

_____

Exercise: Find Alternative Quick Fixes

There will be times when you won't be able to surf the urge. It's okay. You've got options.

Make a list of the different ways you can respond to the trigger. Think about the need you are trying to meet and look at your quick-fix responses in Chapter 2. Identify compelling distractions.

I'm having an urge to use. Instead, I can...

_____   _____

_____   _____

_____   _____

_____   _____

_____   _____

_____   _____

_____   _____

_____   _____

_____   _____

_____   _____

Which response is most aligned with your values?

_____

_____

_____

What do you need in order to commit to the most valued response?

_____

_____

_____

Sources

Corsale, E. & Smithstein, S. (2010). *Taking Back What's Been Stolen.* San Francisco, CA: Pathways Institute Press.

Marlatt, G. A. & Donova, D. M. (2005). *Relapse Prevention: Maintenance Strategies in the Treatment of Addictive Behaviors*. New York, NY: The Guilford Press.

Tatarsky, A. (2002). *Harm Reduction Psychotherapy: A New Treatment for Drug and Alcohol Problems.* Lanham, MD: Rowman & Littlefield Publishers, Inc.

Chapter 15
How Thoughts Impact Addiction

 "The world as we have created it is a process of our thinking. It cannot be changed without changing our thinking."

-Albert Einstein

Now that you understand how emotions and behaviors impact the choices you make with drugs, let's look at the role that thoughts play.

Our thinking, emotions, and behaviors are linked. They influence each other. What you feel affects your thinking which in turn dictates the behavior you engage in. Thoughts can also influence behavior by eliciting emotions. Behavior can lead to feelings that lead to thoughts.

Behaviors, feelings, and thoughts create a triad of factors that feed into each other. Understanding the role that each one plays can help you have a different relationship with drugs. Ultimately this self-knowledge can help you live a more fulfilling life. When you understand yourself, you are more likely to make choices that are aligned with your values.

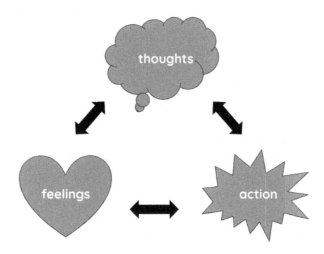

First, let's focus on understanding the relationship between thoughts and emotions.

Bring to mind a pleasant memory from the last year. Maybe you fell in love with someone, got a promotion at your job, went on vacation, or perhaps you ate a really wonderful meal. Notice how recalling the memory stimulates thoughts about the event. The content of the thoughts may include details (*I could feel the sand between my toes and see the palm trees swaying in the distance*) or messaging (*It was such a special treat!*).

Notice how these thoughts stimulate feelings. As you recall the details or talk to yourself about what the event meant to you, you may start to feel happiness, joy, love, warmth, bliss.

Now try this exercise with an unpleasant memory from the last year. Perhaps you got into a fight with a loved one, lost something important, became physically ill, or got a parking ticket. Again, notice the content and messaging in the thoughts. And notice how these thoughts stimulate emotions. You may feel anger, sadness, frustration, guilt, shame.

The thoughts we have cause us to feel certain ways, whether those thoughts reflect reality or not. In the previous exercise you were instructed to recall something that actually happened to you, but you would have a similar experience even if you had been asked to imagine a fictional pleasant or unpleasant memory.

Our thinking doesn't always reflect events as they actually occur. In order to help us cope with the rawness of the real world, sometimes our mind distorts reality. Distorted thinking is something that all humans do. It is adaptive and there is no way to stop it from happening, but we can catch ourselves doing it. Thinking about one's thinking is called metacognition and is a very powerful tool for recovery.

Distorted Thinking

There are many ways that humans distort reality. Here are some of the most common ones:

- Minimizing: shrinking importance inappropriately
    - *Sure I'm doing a good job, it's what I'm supposed to do.*
- All or nothing: seeing things in absolute, black and white, or always-never terms
    - *I'll never change my relationship to drugs.*
    - *I relapsed so all this work has been a waste of time.*
- Jumping to conclusions: assuming an outcome without sufficient evidence
    - *They think I'm stupid.*
    - *My partner didn't smile when I came home tonight. They must be upset with me.*
- Should-ing: criticizing yourself
    - *I should do things right the first time.*
- Personalization: assuming an outcome was your fault or taking things personally
    - *My last therapist wasn't able to help me. I must be a lost cause.*
- Catastrophizing: expecting the absolute worst and inflating the consequences
    - *If I lose control, this will be the end of me.*
    - *If I lose this job it will be the end of my career.*
    - *If I don't use right now, I'm going to die.*

- Filtering: focusing on only positive or negative without considering the whole picture
  - *Look at all the people who don't like me.*
- Emotional reasoning: using your emotions as a reflection of reality rather than a response to a trigger
  - *I feel worthless because I am worthless.*
  - *I feel terrified of flying. Planes must be dangerous.*
  - *I feel angry, that means I'm being treated unfairly.*

Distorted thinking often pops into the mind without warning. This automatic thinking can be hard to catch at first. By tracking automatic distorted thoughts on a daily basis, you will get better at catching and reframing them.

Exercise: Identifying Distorted Thoughts

Make a list of all the distorted thinking you have about your relationship with drugs. Think back to times when distorted thinking has contributed to problematic use. Pay close attention to your thoughts when you experience an urge to use. Keep adding to this list over time and try to write down one distorted thought every day.

Thought Record	
Date	Distorted Thoughts About My Relationship with Drugs

Reality Testing

Once you've identified the distorted thinking associated with your addiction it's time to reality test it. Reality testing just means shifting one's thinking to be more reflective of reality. For example, if you have a distorted thought that sounds like, "My relationship to alcohol doesn't hurt anyone," a reality tested response would sound like, "When I drink too much, I often feel shame about my choices and it causes my loved ones to worry about me."

One method to help you reality test distorted thinking is to play the role of a lawyer. Channel your inner Perry Mason and identify the facts.

My relationship to drugs isn't harmful.

List all the potential harms:
- *When I drink too much I feel hungover*
- *When I use too much coke I get sinus infections*
- *Smoking too much cannabis can lead to lung problems*
- *Meth can have a negative effect on my cardiovascular system*
- *Excessive ketamine use can lead to bladder problems*
- *When I take too much MDMA I feel depressed*
- *NBOMEs have a high risk of overdose*
- *If I take too much DXM I get dizzy*

My addiction only affects me.

List all the people who care about you:
- *My partner says I get verbally abusive when I drink too much*
- *My friends worry that I use coke to cope when I feel sad*
- *My boss has been asking if everything is ok in my personal life*
- *My kids get less attention from me when I'm high*
- *I forget to take my dog for a walk after I've used*

I'll never be able to change my relationship with drugs.

List all the changes you've made, no matter how small:
- *I don't blackout from drinking as often.*
- *I stopped myself from using once.*
- *I'm starting to understand my unmet needs.*
- *I'm setting better boundaries in my relationships.*
- *I'm managing my mental health.*

I should be able to change my behavior on my own.

List all the ways that social support benefits your change process:
- *Talking to friends about my addiction helps me feel less alone with it.*
- *I get good advice from others.*
- *Sharing my weekly goal with someone keeps me accountable.*
- *Spending time with friends is a healthy distraction.*
- *I get support for other things from my community so I can focus on my mental health.*

If I don't use, I'll won't be able to shake this uncomfortable feeling.

List all the ways you can cope with unpleasant emotions:
- *I can surf the emotion.*
- *I feel less badly when I talk to my sister.*
- *Diaphragmatic breathing helps calm me down.*
- *Focusing on work usually distracts me.*
- *Listening to music changes my mood.*
- *I can accept that discomfort is a normal, healthy human experience.*

If I stop using, I won't be able to access my creativity.

List ways to maintain a creativity practice:
- *I can sign up for a class to enhance my skills.*
- *I will dedicate two days of the week solely to creative projects.*
- *Renting a studio keeps me accountable to my creative goals.*
- *I talk about my projects with other creative friends.*
- *I commit to my scheduled creative time, even if creativity is not flowing.*

I won't have any fun if I don't take a little ketamine before clubbing.

List other fun things about clubbing:
- *Dancing*
- *Sharing the experience with friends*
- *Flirting*
- *Music*
- *Meeting new people*
- *Dressing up*

Exercise: Reality Testing

Write down the distorted thoughts you identified in the previous exercise and reality test them. Keep adding to this list and working on this exercise as you identify distorted thinking in the coming weeks and months.

Reality Testing	
Distorted Thought	Reality

Core Beliefs

Distorted thinking isn't limited to addiction. Our mind distorts all of reality and often the way we distort is related to the core beliefs we have about ourselves, others, the world, and the future. Distorted thinking spans from the macro (what you believe about existence) to the micro (how you feel in your own skin).

One way to begin understanding your unique pattern of distortion is to identify themes in your automatic thinking. Just like you practiced writing down all the automatic thoughts you had about your relationship with drugs, write down the automatic thoughts you have throughout the day.

Exercise: Identifying Core Beliefs

Keep a thought record and jot down all the distorted thinking you catch about yourself, other people, your environment, and your future.

Common distorted thoughts might sound like:
- *I'm always late.*
- *No one ever invites me to lunch.*
- *I didn't relapse today, but that's only because I was too busy.*
- *That person thinks I'm a loser.*
- *I'm going to fail this test.*
- *If I go out in public I'm going to have a panic attack.*
- *I must be a failure because I feel like one.*
- *I shouldn't need help.*
- *My loved ones are unhappy because of me.*
- *I can never count on anyone.*
- *I should be doing better in life.*
- *I always mess things up.*
- *I can't handle this.*

Thought Record	
Date	**Distorted Thoughts About Myself, Others, the World, & the Future**

What themes do you notice? These themes speak to the distorted core beliefs you hold. Because you've held these beliefs for a long time, they will be challenging to change. With practice you can develop healthy core beliefs, reduce the frequency of distorted thinking, and engage in problematic behaviors less often.

Sounds great, right? Make sure to set up some rituals for yourself so you can remain committed and accountable to your practice. Dedicate 30 minutes a week to think about your thinking. Set a daily calendar reminder to observe your thoughts for five minutes.

Common maladaptive core beliefs include:
- *I'm unloveable.*
- *Others can't be trusted.*
- *I must be perfect to be accepted.*
- *The world is too unsafe.*
- *I must always be in control.*
- *I'm stupid.*
- *I'm a failure.*
- *I'll always be broken.*
- *Things will never get better.*
- *My needs are too much.*

Exercise: Healthy Core Beliefs

Use the table to write down your distorted core beliefs and identify the healthy core beliefs you'd like to cultivate.

Healthy core beliefs include:
- *I'm just as worthy as others.*
- *I'm a good person.*
- *I am capable.*
- *I have value.*
- *I'm enough.*
- *I strive to do my best.*
- *Mistakes are human.*
- *The world is complicated. I trust myself to navigate it wisely.*
- *Everyone deserves a chance to prove their trustworthiness.*

Core Beliefs	
Distorted Core Belief	**Healthy Core Belief**

Chapter 16
Responsible Drug Use

Now that you've addressed the problematic aspects of your relationship with drugs, let's discuss strategies for cultivating healthy and responsible use.

Set & Setting

Probably the most important tool for responsible drug use is to always consider "set" and "setting" before using. Set refers to your current mindset and setting refers to the environment in which the drug use will take place. Norman Zinberg, MD published the book *Drug, Set, Setting* in the 1980s describing the factors that preclude some people from becoming addicted despite using illicit drugs. *Drug, Set, Setting* has become an important harm reduction tool for many people who use drugs.

To practice responsible use, first consider the drug being ingested:

- What kind of drug is it (stimulant, depressant, dissociative, hallucinogen)?
- What are its effects?
- What is the standard dose?
- What other drugs enhance its effects (this is known as synergy) and which are contraindicated?
- How is it administered?

Drugs can be consumed in various ways: orally, smoked, insufflated (snorting), rectally, intravenous injection, or intramuscular injection. Make sure you understand the risks of your desired route of administration. Choose the least harmful one, if possible.

Inform yourself as much as possible about the drug before taking it. Erowid.org and bluelight.org are reliable and excellent sources of information about drugs. They even have online forums should you have questions about the drug you want to take.

Next, consider the setting. Where will you be taking the drug? What is the environment like? Taking psychedelics at a music festival will be a different experience from taking them alone at home. Will you be around people you know and trust?

Lastly, think about your mindset (this is the part known as set). How has your mood been lately? How about your physical health? Are you stressed out and seeking escape? Are you looking to expand your consciousness? Have you been feeling grief about a recent loss? Are you looking to connect on a deeper level with loved ones?

There's no need to judge your reason for using, but it is imperative that you are intentional about it. Think long and hard about why this choice is important to you. Identify how it aligns with your values.

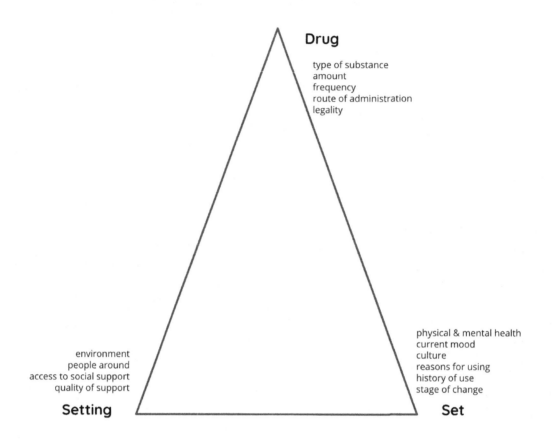

Exercise: Responsible Use Checklist

Use this checklist to help you plan for responsible use. Remember, there is no such thing as safe drug use. All drug use carries risk. Unless you are consuming a regulated drug (like alcohol, nicotine, or cannabis) you can't be certain of its contents or purity.

- ❏ I understand the class of drug I'm taking.
- ❏ I have researched its effects and the standard dose.
- ❏ I've weighed the dose I'm using and if unsure of the source, tested it.
- ❏ I understand the risks of the administration route I've chosen.
- ❏ If I plan on using more than one drug at once, I have researched the potential synergistic and harmful effects of drug combinations.
- ❏ I feel safe in the environment where I will use.
- ❏ People who I trust will be around me or (if using alone) someone knows that I am taking a drug and I have a safety plan.
- ❏ It is appropriate to take this drug given my current mood.
- ❏ It is appropriate to take this drug given my current physical health.

❏   I am taking this drug for reasons that align with my values.

My intention for taking this drug is

_____

_____

_____

By choosing to use this drug, I am honoring my values of

_____

_____

_____

Reducing Harm

There are many harm reduction strategies to implement when using drugs and each drug warrants its own considerations. *Over the Influence* and *Buzzed* are great resources for learning about responsible use of drugs.

Here are some general tips for reducing harm and increasing enjoyment when using drugs:

- Buy less so you use less.
- Lower the frequency and dosage of drugs that have become problematic.
- Choose the least harmful method of administration. Injecting drugs can lead to more harm than snorting or smoking them. If you decide you want to inject, check out the Harm Reduction Coalition's manual *Getting Off Right* to avoid common harms.
- Plan some sober days. Daily use leads to more harm. Try to take at least two or three days off in between.
- Set your own pace and don't let others pressure you into taking more or using more often.
- Keep condoms handy in your pocket or bag. Even if you don't think you'll want to have sex, you might change your mind after using.
- If you are offered drugs, be cautious.
- When trying something for the first time, start with a small amount and wait to see what effect it has on you.
- Know your dealer rather than buying from a stranger. But keep in mind that even a trusted dealer may not know the origin and ingredients of a drug.
- Don't share needles, pipes, straws, or any other equipment.
- NEVER drive while under the influence.
- Educate yourself before combining drugs. *TripSit* makes a reference chart for common drug combinations.

- Test drugs before consuming them. *DanceSafe* sells drug testing kits online. Note that drug tests don't tell you every ingredient in a drug, only whether or not a specific drug is included in the mix.
- If you use opioids be sure to keep naloxone on hand. Get trained on how to administer naloxone in the case of an opioid overdose.

Sources

Zinberg, N. (1986). *Drug, Set, and Setting: The Basis for Controlled Intoxicant Use.* New Haven, CT: Yale University Press.

Recommended Reading

Denning, P. & Little, J. (2017). *Over the Influence* (2nd ed.). New York, NY: The Guilford Press.

https://erowid.org

https://bluelight.org

https://tripsit.me

https://dancesafe.org

Harm Reduction Coalition. (2011). *Getting Off Right: A Safety Manual for Injection Drug Users.* http://harmreduction.org/wp-content/uploads/2011/12/getting-off-right.pdf

Kuhn, C., Swartzwelder, S., and Wilson, W. (2008). *Buzzed: The Straight Facts About the Most Used and Abused Drugs from Alcohol to Ecstasy* (3rd ed.). New York, NY: W.W. Norton & Company.

Chapter 17
Crafting Your Lifestyle

The key to maintaining a healthy relationship with drugs is to also maintain a healthy lifestyle, as it can provide a core stability that will make you more resilient against problematic use. This lifestyle is based on your values and takes time to cultivate. It is not a destination to be reached, but rather a journey with constant detours and rerouting. As your needs change, the strategies used to achieve health will also evolve.

Cultivating a healthy lifestyle requires self-awareness, commitment, and support. It requires you to understand your values, needs, and boundaries. It also requires help from others. A healthy lifestyle is full of meaning, comfort, and joy. This doesn't mean it is free of pain or distress. These are unavoidable truths of human life. But a healthy lifestyle minimizes stress and suffering where possible.

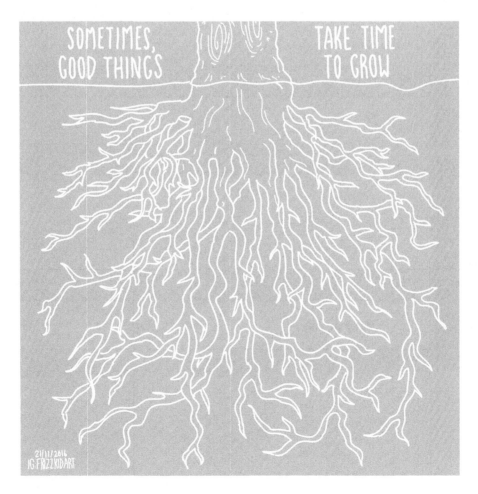

Take an inventory of your current lifestyle. Let's see how well it is functioning, how effective it is at meeting your needs, and how aligned it is with your values.

Exercise: Lifestyle Inventory

Some of these questions may feel like they affirm your life situation, while others may highlight a painful deficit. It's okay! Everyone is on a journey of growth, and awareness is a powerful tool towards positive change.

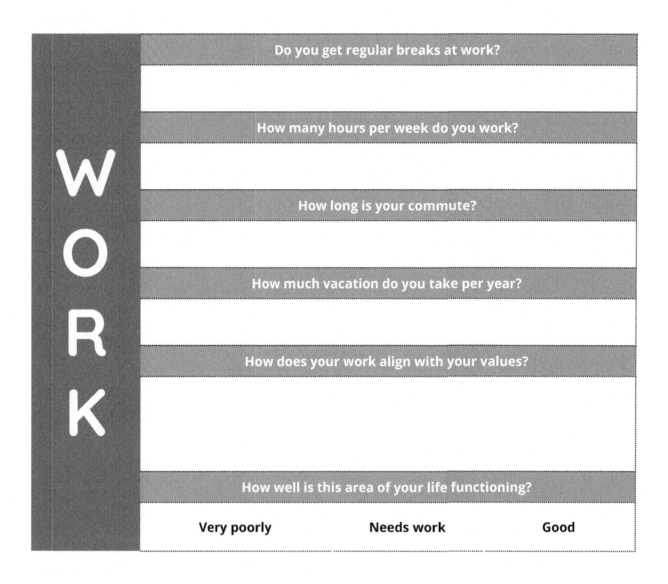

WORK

Do you get regular breaks at work?

How many hours per week do you work?

How long is your commute?

How much vacation do you take per year?

How does your work align with your values?

How well is this area of your life functioning?

Very poorly   Needs work   Good

MONEY

What is your system for maintaining a budget?

How much debt do you owe?

How much money do you save every month?

How are you planning for retirement?

What are your attitudes towards consumerism and materialism?

How well is this area of your life functioning?

Very poorly   Needs work   Good

HEALTH

Are you getting the nutrients you need?

Do you avoid excess sugar and processed foods?

How much water do you drink daily?

How often do you get health screenings?

How often do you visit the dentist?

Have you ever struggled with an eating disorder?

How do you feel about your physical appearance?

How do you educate yourself about healthy habits?

Is there a history of heart disease, diabetes, or cancer in your immediate family?

Do you have chronic illnesses that require regular management?

Do you have access to appropriate medical treatment and medication?

HEALTH cont.

How many hours do you sleep on average?

How much exercise do you get every week?

Which of the following barriers to physical activity do you struggle with?

Lack of time	Social influence	Lack of energy
Lack of willpower	Fear of injury	Lack of skill
Weather conditions	travel	Family obligations

How well is this area of your life functioning?

Very poorly	Needs work	Good

MENTAL HEALTH

Do you have a history of depression, anxiety, bipolar, psychosis, or addiction in your immediate family?

Do you have a chronic mental illness that requires regular management?

How often do you practice meditation or deep breathing?

How do you manage anger?

What is your system for reducing stress?

Do you tend to avoid feelings or do you allow yourself to experience them (even the difficult ones)?

Are you able to identify your feelings?

How do you communicate your feelings to others?

How often do you become overwhelmed by unpleasant emotions?

How well is this area of your life functioning?

Very poorly	Needs work	Good

LEISURE

How much unstructured quiet time do you get per day?

What are your hobbies or passions?

How many hours per week do you dedicate to hobbies?

Are your loved ones supportive of your hobbies?

How well is this area of your life functioning?

Very poorly   Needs work   Good

PARTNERSHIP

How does your current romantic relationship align with values?

Describe your communication style with this person.

How do you resolve conflict in this relationship?

Do you repeatedly put your partner's needs before your own?

Is there emotional abuse or violence?

Do you have sex when you don't want to?

How much quality time do you spend with this person on a weekly basis?

How do you maintain healthy boundaries with your partner?

How well is this area of your life functioning?

Very poorly	Needs work	Good

FAMILY

What is the quality of relationship with your family members?

How are conflicts resolved within the family?

Do you tend to put their needs before your own?

How does your family respond to healthy boundary setting?

Are you the caretaker for an older family member?

How do you get support for your role as caregiver?

How well is this area of your life functioning?

Very poorly	Needs work	Good

PARENTING

What are the joys and challenges of parenting?

How does your community support your parenting?

Describe the relationship with your co-parent.

How do you plan for the financial costs of raising children?

What is your source for information on healthy parenting?

Do your children have special needs or challenges that require regular management?

How many hours of quality time do you get with your family every week?

How well is this area of your life functioning?

Very poorly	Needs work	Good

S O C I A L   L I F E

What do you do for fun with friends?

Where do you fall on the introversion-extroversion spectrum?

Have you ever struggled with social anxiety?

Do you tend to put your friends' needs before your own?

Who do you turn to for support?

How do you resolve conflict with your closest friend?

How much time do you spend with friends on a weekly basis?

How well is this area of your life functioning?

Very poorly	Needs work	Good

H O M E

What is your system for completing household duties?

Do you feel physically comfortable in your home?

Do you have stable housing?

Do you fear for your safety in your neighborhood?

How important are order and cleanliness?

Do you accumulate so many things that it makes your life unmanageable?

How well is this area of your life functioning?

Very poorly	Needs work	Good

MEANING

Do you have religious or spiritual practices that bring meaning to your life? If not, do you wish you did?

Have you ever experienced abuse or oppression from a religious institution?

How much time do you spend in nature?

How often do you experience art, architecture, or music?

How do you express your creativity?

On a weekly basis, how much time do you spend on practices that tune out the outside world and turn your attention inward?

How do you practice kindness?

What are some ways you perform community service?

How well is this area of your life functioning?

Very poorly	Needs work	Good

GROWTH

The following are characteristics of self-actualization as described by Abraham Maslow. Self-actualizing is reaching one's fullest potential.

Are you able to judge situations correctly and honestly? Can you accept the good, bad, highs, and lows of life? Are you able to discern between reality and distorted perception? Are you sensitive to fakery and dishonesty?

Are you able to accept yourself, others, and the world as they are? Are you able to accept responsibility for who you are? Are you able to accept your flaws?

How often are you spontaneous? Do you get hung up on how others think you should be? Do you feel capable of doing what feels good and natural to you?

How much energy do you put into problems outside yourself? How often do you focus on your problems?

GROWTH cont.

How much time do you need for yourself on a weekly basis? Are you comfortable being around your loved ones without needing to communicate?

How autonomous and independent are you? Do you feel capable of doing things for yourself and making decisions on your own? Do you believe in yourself?

Do you find pleasure in the simple things? How often do you experience gratitude?

Have you ever had a peak experience of transcendence? How often do you feel in tune with the world around you?

GROWTH cont.

How often do you have the experience of feeling connected to all of humanity? Are you aware of and sensitive to the people around you?

Do you consider your relationships to be deep, profound, and meaningful?

Do you have a democratic attitude towards others? Do you respect people of all races, classes, sexual orientations, gender expressions, and ableness? Are you able to recognize the strengths and weaknesses in others?

Are you able to discern between means and ends? Can you tell the difference between good and evil? Are you careful to never confuse the two in order to avoid hurting yourself and others?

GROWTH cont.

Do you have a good sense of humor? Do you laugh at the expense of others?

Do you value expression of your creativity?

Do you resist conformity to the mainstream culture?

How well is this area of your life functioning?

Very poorly	Needs work	Good

SEXUALITY

Do you enjoy sex?

Are you having as much sex as you'd like?

How do you communicate your sexual needs to partners?

What is your understanding of sexual reproductive systems?

Which safe sex practices do you use?

Which forms of contraception do you use?

What is your general attitude towards sex?

Are you a survivor of sexual trauma?

Do you feel shame about sex or masturbation?

Do you ever use sex as a means of coping with unpleasant emotions?

Have you ever experienced discrimination because of your sexual orientation?

How well is this area of your life functioning?

Very poorly	Needs work	Good

CHANGE

How do you typically respond to the major life events below?

Major illnesses, injuries, or surgeries

Changes with type, frequency, or duration of work

Trouble with coworkers, boss

Retirement

Loss of work

Major change in living conditions

Marriage or divorce

Pregnancy or adoption

Child leaving home

CHANGE cont.

Death of loved one

Beginning or ending school

Change in political or religious beliefs

Vacation

Major personal achievement

Major change in finances

Loss or damage of personal property

How well is this area of your life functioning?

Very poorly   Needs work   Good

D E A T H

What was your first experience of death?

How was death spoken about when you were a child?

What was your childhood conception of death?

What is your current attitude about death?

How often do you think about your own death?

If you could choose, when would you die?

What aspect of death do you most fear?

To what extent are you interested in having your image survive after your own death?

If you had a choice, what kind of death would you prefer?

DEATH cont.

How important are mourning and grief rituals?

How would you like your body disposed of after you die?

What kind of funeral would you prefer?

What would you like to learn, change, or do before you die?

If you were diagnosed with a terminal illness, who should be the one to tell you that you are dying?

Do you have a will?

Have you identified your advance medical directives and assigned a loved one to be your advocate?

If given the choice, where would you like to die?

How well is this area of your life functioning?

Very poorly	Needs work	Good

Ponder This...

Which set of questions was the most difficult to answer?

_____

_____

_____

What does this inventory tell you about areas of your lifestyle that need to change?

_____

_____

_____

What do you need in order to make the necessary changes?

_____

_____

_____

Sources

Corsale, E. & Smithstein, S. (2010). _Taking Back What's Been Stolen._ San Francisco, CA: Pathways Institute Press.

Chapter 18
Create Meaning in Your Life

Having a better relationship with drugs is only one step towards cultivating a fulfilling life. Part of the journey involves knowing yourself better — understanding your values, knowing your wants and needs, and honoring your boundaries. These practices will help you meet your fullest potential. When you can live in harmony with your values, respect yourself and others, and commit to these practices, a meaningful and satisfying life will follow.

Roger Walsh, MD has been researching wellbeing over the last 30 years and has found the following practices "essential for anyone who would live wisely, love wholeheartedly, mature fully, and contribute effectively."

Live Ethically

Make a commitment to live in line with your values. Honor what you believe to be right versus wrong. Treat others with respect. If you violate your values, you will likely feel guilt or shame. When you make choices that knowingly hurt others you may also feel guilt or shame. You may stop yourself from making these kinds of choices because you don't want to experience "bad karma." Karma is the psychological residue of one's actions. If one feels shame or guilt about an action the resulting psychological residue will fester and create suffering. Avoid unnecessary suffering by evaluating your choices based on the impact they have on yourself and others.

> "Whatever you do, you do to yourself."
>
> — Buddha

Transform Emotions

Practice equanimity (balance of mind) and compassion with unpleasant emotions. Remind yourself that pain is a normal, healthy part of the human experience. Stop yourself from judging this experience in yourself and in others. Observe it instead. Notice how it takes shape in the body and mind. Practice non-attachment and let go of expectations. Study mindfulness to train your mind to remain even, calm, and balanced in the face of difficult situations.

Cultivate emotional intelligence for yourself and others. Get to know your emotional self well. Make a habit of identifying and valuing your feeling states, especially the painful ones. Communicate your feelings assertively when appropriate. Practice accurately identifying emotions in others. Hone your wise mind to effectively use emotional and rational information to influence your thinking and behaviors. Manage your emotions so they don't flood and overwhelm you.

Redirect Motivation

Your human mind will crave and desire unhealthy things. When you notice a craving for something harmful or outside your value system, see if you can identify the underlying need without judgment. Then transform it into motivation for something healthy that also meets the need. Let your values guide your choices.

Train Your Attention

Controlling attention is difficult for our human brains. We are constantly distracted by various stimuli in our environment and especially so when we have access to smartphones. By practicing sustained attention we can eventually cultivate positive emotional states and healthy motives. Concentration and attention facilitate awareness of self and others, connecting us to deep wants and needs. Create a daily routine that involves sustained focus for at least 10 minutes.

Refine Your Awareness

By observing your inner world through mindfulness and sustained attention, you allow unconscious experiences to come into the light. With this practice, awareness has the potential to heal. Observing once-hidden fears, criticism, and beliefs removes their power over us. When we remain aware, we are unable to avoid, repress, or dissociate from our truths. Share your inner experience with someone you trust. Journal regularly. Cultivate a self-reflective ritual and request feedback from others. We all have blind spots and we need others to help us see them.

Cultivate Wisdom

Seek to understand the varied and often contradictory processes of life. Discern between wisdom and knowledge. Knowledge is the information gained from study, observation, and research. Wisdom is ability to discern and judge when knowledge is accurate and how it applies to your life.

Allow yourself to ponder big existential questions — what it means to be human, the purpose of life, the meaning of death. Learn from wise teachers and mentors.

Serve Others

Helping and giving to others can be a transformative experience. Often people experience a helper's high and report reduced feelings of anger or longing after engaging in a generous act. Service to others increases feelings of joy, compassion, and connection. Regularly participate in service to others in your community. Train yourself to experience sympathetic joy — a feeling of joy that comes from observing joy in others. Just as laughter or yawning can be contagious, one can experience a vicarious joy from others.

Sources

Walsh, R. (1999). *Essential Spirituality: The 7 Central Practices to Awaken Heart and Mind*. New York, NY: John Wiley & Sons, Inc.

You did it!

Congratulations on completing the workbook! Take a moment to acknowledge all the hard work and effort you've put into having a different relationship with drugs. You've learned many new things, taken steps towards new behaviors, and made changes in your relationships. You deserve to feel proud and accomplished. Go ahead, brag! Let your loved ones and support system know about this accomplishment.

Take some time to reflect on your work throughout this book. Go back and read through your responses to the exercises and questions. Reflect on your growth over time. Highlight the practices and skills that were most helpful to you and integrate them into your routine.

Appendix A
Resources for Professionals

This list of resources is recommended for healing professionals who want to increase their understanding of harm reduction psychotherapy. It is strongly recommended that you also seek consultation and training with experts in the field.

Bowen, S., Chawla, N., & Marlatt, G.A. (2011). *Mindfulness-Based Relapse Prevention for Addictive Behaviors: A Clinician's Guide*. New York, NY: The Guilford Press.

Denning, P., & Little, J. (2012). *Practicing Harm Reduction Psychotherapy* (2nd ed.). New York, NY: The Guilford Press.

Hayes, S.C. & Levin, M. (2012). *Mindfulness and Acceptance for Addictive Behaviors: Applying Contextual CBT to Substance Abuse and Behavioral Addictions*. Oakland, CA: New Harbinger.

Hester, R.K. & Miller, W.R. (2002). *Handbook of Alcoholism Treatment Approaches: Effective Alternatives* (3rd ed.). Boston, MA: Allyn and Bacon.

Miller, W. R., Forcehimes, A. F., & Zweben, A. (2011). *Treating addiction: A guide for professionals*. New York, NY: The Guilford Press.

Sobell, M.B & Sobell, L.C. (1993). *Problem Drinkers: Guided Self-Change Treatment*. New York, NY: The Guilford Press

Sobell, L. C. & Sobell, M. B. (2011). *Group therapy for substance use disorders: A motivational cognitive-behavioral approach*. New York, NY: The Guilford Press.

Tatarsky, A. (2002). *Harm Reduction Psychotherapy: A New Treatment for Drug and Alcohol Problems*. Lanham, MD: Rowman & Littlefield Publishers, Inc.

Appendix B
Worksheets

You may find that you want to work on the exercises in this workbook for an extended period of time. Extra copies of some of the exercises are included here should you want to make copies.

Finding Alternatives

Identify alternatives to drug use that fulfill your unmet need. In the first column of the table list all the gains (or benefits) from using. In the second column list other ways you can gain the benefit. Don't feel limited by activities or external coping strategies. Identify your internal resources as well. In the last column, indicate whether the alternative is a long-term solution (LT) or quick fix (QF). Aim for alternatives in each category.

Alternative Strategies		
What I gain from using	Other ways to gain the benefit	LT/QF

A Month of Healthy Communication

1. Practice talking about yourself for a week. Start as many statements as possible with "I feel," "I need," and "I want."

	"I" Statements		
Date	"I feel" statements	"I need" statements	"I want" statements

2. Practice active listening for a week. Keep a log for each day noting who you listened to, the topic, how long you listened, and how it felt to listen without responding.

Active Listening				
Date	I listened to...	talk about...	for...	and I felt...

3. Practice mirroring for a week. Start with easy, superficial topics. Mirror your co-worker after they complain about work stress. Mirror a loved one after they vent about chores or traffic. Gradually work your way up to more difficult conversations over the course of the week.

Mirroring				
Date	I mirrored...	and it was...		
		easy	challenging	very difficult
		easy	challenging	very difficult
		easy	challenging	very difficult
		easy	challenging	very difficult
		easy	challenging	very difficult
		easy	challenging	very difficult
		easy	challenging	very difficult
		easy	challenging	very difficult
		easy	challenging	very difficult
		easy	challenging	very difficult
		easy	challenging	very difficult
		easy	challenging	very difficult
		easy	challenging	very difficult
		easy	challenging	very difficult
		easy	challenging	very difficult
		easy	challenging	very difficult
		easy	challenging	very difficult
		easy	challenging	very difficult
		easy	challenging	very difficult
		easy	challenging	very difficult
		easy	challenging	very difficult

4. Practice nonviolent communication for a week. Again, start with easier topics and work your way up to more difficult or uncomfortable conversations over the week.

Nonviolent Communication				
Date	Hurtful Event	Feelings	Needs/Values	Request

Get to Know Your Pain

The next time you feel a painful emotion, take the time to get to know it. Name all the emotions you are feeling. Rate the pain on a scale from one to ten, one being uncomfortable and ten being extreme anguish or despair. If the pain registers at five or below continue with the exercise. If it registers above six, practice exercises from the mindfulness chapter until the pain decreases to a manageable level.

Pain Log		
Date	Unpleasant emotion(s)	Intensity (1=uncomfortable, 10=anguish)
		1 2 3 4 5 6 7 8 9 10
	Bodily Sensations	Thoughts during Pain
Date	Unpleasant emotion(s)	Intensity (1=uncomfortable, 10=anguish)
		1 2 3 4 5 6 7 8 9 10
	Bodily Sensations	Thoughts during Pain
Date	Unpleasant emotion(s)	Intensity (1=uncomfortable, 10=anguish)
		1 2 3 4 5 6 7 8 9 10
	Bodily Sensations	Thoughts during Pain

Anger Tracking

Keep a log of every time you feel angry and note how angry you felt. Rate the anger a "1" if you felt annoyed, "2" if you felt angry, and "3" if you felt rage. Next, log what made you angry and how you responded. Finally, consider whether you could have responded differently and what a better response would have been.

Anger Log		
Date	Trigger	Intensity
		1—annoyed 2—angry 3—enraged
	Actual Response	Better Response
Date	Trigger	Intensity
		1—annoyed 2—angry 3—enraged
	Actual Response	Better Response
Date	Trigger	Intensity
		1—annoyed 2—angry 3—enraged
	Actual Response	Better Response

Stress Log

Track incidents of stress and note the trigger. Rate the intensity from slightly stressful to very stressful. At the end of the tracking period, identify the areas where you can eliminate stress.

Stress Log		
Date	Trigger	Intensity
		slightly stressful | stressful | very stressful
	How can I eliminate or reduce this stressor?	
Date	Trigger	Intensity
		slightly stressful | stressful | very stressful
	How can I eliminate or reduce this stressor?	
Date	Trigger	Intensity
		slightly stressful | stressful | very stressful
	How can I eliminate or reduce this stressor?	
Date	Trigger	Intensity
		slightly stressful | stressful | very stressful
	How can I eliminate or reduce this stressor?	

Combat Shame-Based Thinking

Make a list of the self-critical thoughts you experience when feeling shame. Write a counter argument in the column on the right.

From Self-Loathing to Self-Love	
Self-Critical Thinking	**Self-Compassionate Counter**

Urge Tracking

Tracking urges will help you start making connections to triggers and unmet needs. It also gives you feedback about how often you are experiencing urges and how intense they are.

Urge Tracking					
Date	**How long did it last?**	**What triggered it?**	**How intense was it?**		
			mild	moderate	severe
			mild	moderate	severe
			mild	moderate	severe
			mild	moderate	severe
			mild	moderate	severe
			mild	moderate	severe
			mild	moderate	severe
			mild	moderate	severe
			mild	moderate	severe
			mild	moderate	severe
			mild	moderate	severe
			mild	moderate	severe
			mild	moderate	severe
			mild	moderate	severe
			mild	moderate	severe
			mild	moderate	severe
			mild	moderate	severe
			mild	moderate	severe
			mild	moderate	severe
			mild	moderate	severe
			mild	moderate	severe

Relapse Reflection Sheet

Which self-compassion strategies can I practice right now?

_____

_____

What was the underlying unmet need that got the cycle started?

_____

_____

Why is that need important?

_____

_____

_____

Why is it important to make a different choice next time I have an urge to use?

_____

_____

_____

Which values do I violate when I use drugs problematically?

_____

_____

Which values do I honor when I resist urges to use?

_____

_____

Fill out the cycle.

Trigger	
Craving	
Fantasy	
Urge	
Distorted Thinking	
Planning	
High Risk Situation	
Evaluation	

Where did I miss opportunities to take a detour?

_____

_____

_____

What choices do I want to make differently next time?

_____

_____

_____

Find Alternative Quick Fixes

There will be times when you won't be able to surf the urge. Make a list of the different ways you can respond to the trigger. Think about the need you are trying to meet and look at your quick-fix responses in Chapter 2. Identify compelling distractions.

I'm having an urge to use. Instead, I can...

_____   _____

_____   _____

_____   _____

_____   _____

_____   _____

_____   _____

_____   _____

_____   _____

_____   _____

Which response is most aligned with your values?

_____

_____

_____

What do you need in order to commit to the most valued response?

_____

_____

_____

Identifying Distorted Thoughts

Make a list of all the distorted thinking you have about your relationship with drugs.

Thought Record	
Date	**Distorted Thoughts About My Relationship with Drugs**

Reality Testing

Write down the distorted thoughts you identified in the previous exercise and reality test them.

Reality Testing	
Distorted Thought	Reality

Identifying Core Beliefs

Keep a thought record and jot down all the distorted thinking you catch about yourself, other people, your environment, and your future.

Thought Record	
Date	**Distorted Thoughts About Myself, Others, the World, & the Future**

Healthy Core Beliefs

Use the table to write down your distorted core beliefs and identify the healthy core beliefs you'd like to cultivate.

Core Beliefs	
Distorted Core Belief	**Healthy Core Belief**

Responsible Use Checklist

Use this checklist to help you plan for responsible use. Remember, there is no such thing as safe drug use. All drug use carries risk. Unless you are consuming a regulated drug (like alcohol, nicotine, or cannabis) you can't be certain of its contents or purity.

- ❏ I understand the class of drug I'm taking.
- ❏ I have researched its effects and the standard dose.
- ❏ I've weighed the dose I'm using and if unsure of the source, tested it.
- ❏ I understand the risks of the administration route I've chosen.
- ❏ If I plan on using more than one drug at once, I have researched the potential synergistic and harmful effects of drug combinations.
- ❏ I feel safe in the environment where I will use.
- ❏ People who I trust will be around me or (if using alone) someone knows that I am taking a drug and I have a safety plan.
- ❏ It is appropriate to take this drug given my current mood.
- ❏ It is appropriate to take this drug given my current physical health.
- ❏ I am taking this drug for reasons that align with my values.

My intention for taking this drug is

_____

_____

_____

By choosing to use this drug, I am honoring my values of

_____

_____

_____

Made in the USA
Coppell, TX
24 June 2021